THE MANY USES OF MINT

.
New and Selected Poems 1998-2018

By the same author

Instrumentality (2004)
Wanton Textiles (2006)
Language For A New Century (2008)
Voluptuous Bristle (2010)
Seamless Matter (2010)
Deepening Groove (2011)
What Else Could it Be (2015)
The Autobiography Of A Goddess (2016)
Durable Transit (2018)

Contents

Homage

Pataphysics

Singularities

Voyages

Post-pastoral

Carnal Nature

Phrase and Contour

Introduction
by Arundhathi Subramanian

Engorged with image, thick, viscous and churning, Ravi Shankar's poems have the density of mercury as well as its fluidity and mobility. They allow for the gradual accumulation of idea and a welter of tangential detail, gathering form and momentum and a gait all their own. These are not poems of distillation as much as poems of accretion.

The energy is visceral. The language is restless, hungry for surprise, the register swinging between the formal and the demotic (both American and Indian). Underlying this is an almost voluptuous need to embrace myth, history, metaphysics and pop culture, and bring all of it into a single book, and sometimes a single poem. This is matched by an alertness to form—with references ranging from the Bop to the *pada*—making for a playful, stylistically supple poetry.

As one reads, one begins to realise the logic at work. It is a logic fuelled by the human impulse to gather and make sense of all the world's abundance and seeming surplus—an impulse to devour, to leave nothing out. A logic based on the premise that the journey of poetry is riverine and deeply democratic, assimilating tradition and modernity, past and present, east and west, silt and plastic, 'sublime' and 'scatological', classicism and kitsch, without discrimination.

Its pace might sometimes be slowed by such assimilation but not its belief in the inevitability of the journey oceanward. Ravi Shankar's poems have the quality of Ganga in Benaras—sometimes darkly opaque, but never stagnant, always lurching towards some promise of expansion and illumination.

There is an unmistakable philosophical curiosity which makes the poems articulate a need, on the one hand, for resolution. And so, the poet turns, one might say, to the poetic enterprise (as Andal, the Tamil woman mystic he translates, might to her Vishnu) to loosen 'the braids of reason/ until I am an untied string without a knot, united as wave and postulate. Concluded.'

On the other hand, there is no easy resolution. In this lurching journey through insomniac metros (where 'burnt-out taxis rust like lozenges on a tongue of rain') and the 'wending road towards the sea's terminal blues', through 'sinuously wound sentences/laden with polysyllables' and the curiosity about 'gradations of silence' in unoccupied rooms, through the 'cool smoothness' of porcelain plates and the muscular blessing of everyday objects ('Because before the invention of the pump, there was one less way to understand the human heart'), the poetry asks some old questions about being human.

There are no facile answers. And the verbal largesse, or the 'over-empurpling' impulse (that the poet is only too aware of) takes away none of the puzzlement of these questions. These are questions about time, mortality, fate, meaning, and how to live as that creature of perennial in-betweenness—forged, in the poet's words, 'from reptile, neuron and pure want'.

Where does an hour go, the poet wonders? And what is 'this brokenness that bleeds prayer'? And how do we understand 'the human need to enact primal dramas/ even when the act perpetuates a cycle of abuse'? And how does one give up 'the obsession for control' that makes us long to name everything that we hear?

Indeed, the poet is aware that his swathe of word and image can never capture the beguiling and mysterious materiality of the world around him. There are 'secrets' that will not yield simply because there is 'a knife to pry' them open 'and vinegar to serve'. In fact it is probably only when 'the urge to possess' subsides, the poet intuits, that one can access deeper truths, and 'plunge headfirst into shimmering water'.

In one of these poems, the poet writes, 'We colour our language, Wallace Stevens wrote to Elsie Moll/ And Truth, being white, becomes blotched in transmission.'

Ravi Shankar's poetry is emphatically not white. It is highly coloured, often purple. Unapologetically, deliberately, flagrantly so. It evokes not the limpidity of water but the rich, ferrous animality of blood—now myth and concept, now spluttering wetness.

Consider, in fact, his evocation of blood in a poem: 'marrow-sprung, eucharistic fount, black/pudding beaten in a bucket, kept/from coagulating, final taboo sopped/in a tampon or gargling from a slit/ carotid artery'.

In penetrating, unflinching portraits such as these, the concrete and abstract are so integrally wedded that language attains that quality of 'true strangeness and psychic resonance' to which the poet aspires.

Here is poetry that seeks whiteness without denying its love of the polychromatic. That wonders about an ultimate truth without denying its fascination with the wildly plural. It is unafraid to roil, gargle, splutter, sop, drench, and still ache for a tranquil harbour. To plunge into a verbal deluge and still aspire—as one poem so evocatively puts it— to the condition of 'a single waterdrop loosed from/ a lotus petal, spreading drowsy circles in a lake'.

Homage

All goes onward and outward, nothing collapses.
—Walt Whitman

The Utopian

Despite everything, no one can dictate who you are to other people.
—Prince

Dear Prince, in whatever purple astral energy field
you're orbiting—a true glyph now, genderless,

a pure stringless guitar solo ringing with harmonics—
you must have felt the love in the streets from Brixton

to Paisley Park, your many fans dancing out their grief,
lighting candles, leaving snapdragons and tribute letters.

I remember borrowing 'Purple Rain' on cassette tape
in middle school, marvelling, even before I had popped

it in my Walkman, how someone could pull off sexy
and slightly sinister while wearing a high-collared shirt

under a purple suit. On a rock album with a floral border!
You conflated oppositions, opened pores in boundaries,

married electro-funk and gospel to R&B and new wave,
were a suggestive, elfin Lord Byronesque sexual epicurean

who rocked a bouffant, ruffled crop top, and bell-bottoms
(assless please!), all while being a born-again Christian.

Black and intergalactic. Male, newly. Not really camp,
but not in earnest either. You must come from the future,

where music will manifest our identities as polyphonically
as the timbres from a keyboard synthesiser that vibrates

like a horn and a waterfall at the same time.
Where we will not suffer for where or to whom we were born.

Blue Circus (1950)

Mine alone is the land that exists in my soul/I enter
it without a passport like I do my own home–
—Marc Chagall

Polymorphous saturation
              oh blue
        space, river without banks
              speculum mundi
        there's a cock in the corner
                    banging a drum
        fish with a sly eye
head a bed for supple coupling
              horse in green, coquette
                    lovingly decapitated
        by cerulean shadow
              mane preened
                          cooping up a man
                    delirious moon on violin
        flecked orb, yellow orchestral
                          depthless dancing
              to horn, cello, accordion
        ring-wrangling Mediterranean nymph
                    oh blue
                    lumière liberté
              in a diagonal swath
        a trapeze-artist swims
              upside down, rouged
                          peacock crowned
              belly round, breasts round
                    like a prayer
              that sometimes ends
                          in laughter

The Acorn and the Hungry King

He, in sleep, in imagination, dreams of feasts, closes his
mouth on vacancy, grinds tooth on tooth,
exercises his gluttony on insubstantial food, and, instead
of a banquet, fruitlessly eats the empty air.
—Ovid's Metamorphoses, Bk VIII:777-842
(translated by A.S. Kline)

The voice inside the oak sings a high tannic note,
bitter and herbaceous like squashing a sodden

teabag on your tongue until your throat contracts
in revulsion. Those who say its song rounds out

a good sherry, ignore repressed memories of blood
inside the wood, the trauma of the swung axe blade

in Ceres' coppery grove where the Dryads once held
their ancient sacred dances, writhing under votive

tablets and garland wreaths. Bite into an acorn,
and you can taste the faint sweat of those nymphs,

before the aftertaste curdles your stomach with fire.
Desire, the Buddhists advise, *taṇhā* that Pali word,

remains unquenchable, bottomless, a belly ravaged
by famine, like the curse that befell old Erysichthon,

the Thessalian king, when he felled the massive oak,
then fell himself, first ear-sick, then heart-sick,

then forever ravenous, munching the air to breathe,
swallowing whole olives, pit and all, sucking honey

from the bees' hives and milk from the very udders
of his royal cows. The more he devoured, the more

he had to devour, but it was like pitching drachmas
into the Aegean, if the coins were wholly immaterial

and the ocean infinite. He drained each amphora,
only to grow thirstier. He ate until he had his fill,

and he never had his fill. Finally, he began to gnaw
on himself, beginning with his digits, then his hands,

then his very arms up to the elbow and beyond,
crunching bones and sinew. Isn't that the meaning

of craving? The nature of addiction? The hunger
sunk deep inside of you that tries and tries and tries

and tries, but can't get no satisfaction? The dead man,
as a living man, devours a dead man, himself, still

alive, but slowly, surely, dying in excruciating agony.
That's us burning coal and hacking down rainforests.

That's us at the turn of the millennium. Think of him
next time you order a particularly oaky chardonnay.

Thomas Jefferson in Kathmandu

Experience hath shewn, that even under the best forms of government,
those entrusted with power have, in time, and by slow operations,
perverted it into tyranny.
—*Thomas Jefferson, Preamble to a* Bill for the More General
Diffusion of Knowledge *(1778)*

Packed in Thamel into a beat-up tempo, that minivan
    which serves as public transportation in Nepal,
        I'm thumbing your visage on a nickel near the tan

faces of seekers and trekkers, the various people
    of foreign descent who throng the dusty road
        in saffron shirts and rudraksha malas, the steeple

up ahead really a stupa where we stop to unload
    passengers and accept others. Here, I think of you
        TJ, in the faux-Gilbert Stuart portrait that stood

smelling of agar from petri dishes plus an old gym shoe
    odour that never seemed to dissipate from the halls
        of my high school named for you where I went through

facial hair, trigonometry, punk rock, soccer balls,
    SATs, angst, in short the whole gamut of adolescent
        failure and triumph. Now, standing in front of stalls

selling Himalayan masks, frozen in poses of pent
    up animal rage and wood-carved rictuses of wrath,
        I remember how many long hours I once had spent

under your unnoticed gaze, working on some math
        problem or pining over the redhead I was smitten
                with, carrying my dog-eared copy of Sylvia Plath,

dreaming myself a writer before I had even written
        a stanza worth rereading. It would be much later
                at the University you built where I'd be bitten

by the bug properly, a sensation made ever greater
        in the walks I would take traversing your serpentine
                walls, alone, at home in my own mind the way a crater

gives shape to a surface by suggesting what's unseen,
        what might have been once, still what is yet to come.
                I traced the rim of my own unknowing, still so green

but ambitious, questioning everything, trying to shun
        nothing, striking together stones to try to make a fire
                that would burn brighter and deeper than a twinning sun.

Here now is Chitipathi the skeletal lord of the Funeral Pyre
        and Mahakala, the great black one, personal tutelary
                of Kubla Khan, with flared nostrils, bared fangs and ire

to spare. And here you are on your plantation, Mulberry
        Row, where slaves worked as smiths, joiners, weavers,
                carpenters and hostlers, each of whom has a story

untold on unmarked graves or in your writings. Grievers
        mourned your death on Independence Day but of them,
                what? Here I am in Alderman Library working levers

of the elevator moving in half-floors slow as phlegm
　　　　seeping down a basin drain. Here you are in Paris wearing
　　　　　　　　yarn stockings, velveteen breaches, the exquisite hem

of your waistcoat like wild honeysuckle baring
　　　　subtle blossoms. Here are all the dark bodies going
　　　　　　　　into ground after a lifetime of labour and you staring

from Mount Rushmore, me from under the flowing
　　　　rim of the Annapurna mountains. Here are the Bill
　　　　　　　　of Rights, where Sally Hemmings does her light sewing.

I'm on the other side of the world and still
　　　　can't see clearly what has succeeded and what failed
　　　　　　　　in the grand American experiment. I eat my fill,

no prayer bowl to beg from, yet have been jailed
　　　　and bailed out, slurred, even refused service at a diner
　　　　　　　　250 years after you were born. I know I'm not nailed

to a cross, but why is it that I feel so much finer
　　　　and more contented in a country ruled by Maoists
　　　　　　　　and Marxists than I do in the democratic, designer

shining city on the hill where all the Taoists,
　　　　Hindus, and Buddhists I'm meeting want to move
　　　　　　　　to regardless, *to start new lives in the USA*? How is it

possible that the Newari dancers' ancient groove
　　　　feels more timely than twerking, that I'd rather eat
　　　　　　　　dosas and dal than haute cuisine? No need to prove

an answer to those questions as they're mine to read
　　　　and puzzle out, but grown from a seed planted
　　　　　　　　at your plantation into a towering crop I now need

heed. Democracy is a fine ideal yet to be supplanted,
    but does it coexist with capitalism? Today I was told
        a Nepalese proverb which might be loosely translated

as 'cumin in an elephant's mouth', meaning how all gold
    shines valueless next to our own nothingness, how the priceless
        figs we hunger for are impossible to be bought or sold.

I've secreted the nickel now into the folds of a torn dress
    a woman with child uses to collect rupees. She is our
        mother from another life and you and I are no less,

no more than brothers. If even in this late hour,
    honesty is the first chapter in the book of wisdom,
        then its epilogue must be compassion. Not power.

The Third of May (1814)

It is not easy to retrain the instantaneous and
transitory design that issues from the imagination.
—*Francisco De José Y Lucientes*

When they come for you, Cossack-capped,
in lockstep, carrying the black eye of death
against their shoulders, how will you react?
Bending low, earthwards, hands interlaced
in supplication, eyes pleading for mercy
from the uniforms striding towards you,
or brandishing a fist, jaw clenched,
resolute with bright inflections of hatred?
With your face deep in your hands, blinded,
telling yourself *this can't be happening,*
no, my life was not meant to end like this,
or hiding behind someone, anyone, hoping
that somehow you're missed, that they run
out of ammo, that your neighbor will take
the bullet meant for you and you'll escape?
Or will you fling out your arms like a father
receiving his son home from traveling abroad,
elated to know an end to all journeying?

The Flock's Reply to the Passionate Shepherd

After Christopher Marlowe

Marooned upon this grassy knoll,
We wander lost from vale to pole,
Our wooly backs resemble thorn,
It's been a while since we've been shorn.

You waste much time trying to woo
That nymph who never will see you.
Since it's a shepherd that you are,
You're better off courting a star.

But over here, your loyal flock
Needs no clasp, no precious rock
To follow you from field to field:
If love's your need, we can but yield.

Have you not heard us cry and bleat
When you approach us, then retreat?
We miss your orders and your laugh,
We even miss your clouting staff.

Save those gowns made of our wool,
No need to make belts or to pull
Posies from the hillside's crease—
That nymph is what we call a tease.

Just as the hours wing away,
There are some sheep that love to play:
If such delights your mind might move
Then live with us and be our love.

The Two Fridas (1939)

wave – ray – earth – red – I am.
—*Frida Kahlo*

corseted heart

raison d'être et de souffrir

through the veins of air

a twined system of tubes

convalescent songs

snakes unembroidered feather

under bronze skin paling

turquoise *retablos*

how red corridos sound

miracle that courses

through stuccoed adobes

transparent as buried ice

sunken Tehuana

bone-dry blizzards

watery lips slightly pursed

brandied blood

Diego

Diego

snip

snip

snip

once a loosed rod slashed

gold flake patina wafted

no sufficient bandage

left body bent immobile

the shape of glacial patience

that has no explicable scrim

but convulsive vibrations

not sick but broken

in voluptuous transience

a syringe or ferrule or nipple

strings of bone torn

hand in hand until the end

leaving the flesh joyful

drill bit to pierce skin

from a fractured package

mujer tan cansada

bundled alone in blue house

birthing a disembodied eye

no unexposed surface

skies mottled with storm

a taint stained yellow

a brush dreams of being

the self other than itself

leaved by a knife in two

appears shimmering in air

never, never to return—

Architect attacked by a Goshawk, or the Unsilent Night

It comes from everywhere and at the same time you can't
pinpoint where any of it is coming from.
—*Phil Kline*

Turns out there's an aggressive bird in the woods
by the farthest studio that must have just given birth,
because it's patrolling the treetops for intruders,
like artists from Brooklyn sauntering to glimpse
ferns & deer scat, unaware that mama will swoop
like a scythe at their head & in the case of the architect,
draw blood from his scalp. When he tells the story
at dinner, he's surprisingly calm though the evocation
of the rasp of talons sends shudders through half
the table. Wear a helmet next time, someone brays.
Wave a stick, someone else proffers. I want to go
on a hawk-walk, mourns another, nothing ever happens
to me. Come to Atlanta in December, says the composer,
& you too can be part of something cool. He describes
putting on Phil Kline's ambient auditory perambulation
caroling tour through the streets, participants
carrying boom boxes and amplifiers that play one
of four different parts that interact with each other
as they walk through the city, New York City originally,
going from Washington Square Park to Tomkins Square,
but now transposed to cities all over the world.
Something about the swirling sounds, chimes
& warbling bells reflecting off buildings into open
spaces, intermingling with street noise as the sound
moves through a mapped route—always the same,
yet different every year—in each new place the piece
is performed, recaptures the physical mystery

of inhabiting place by moving through it,
leaving like a wisp of smoke, an ephemeral trail
of reverberations that receding into memory
takes on the aural dimensions of the sublime.
At a nearby table, the architect is touching
the back of his head & saying that fucking hawk.

Lines on a Skull

An erasure of Lord Byron's 'Lines Inscribed
Upon a Cup Formed from a Skull' into haiku

Start spirit; behold
the skull. A living head loved
earth. My bones resign

the worm, lips to hold
sparkling grape's slimy circle,
shape of reptile's food.

Where wit shone of shine,
when our brains are substitute,
like me, with the dead,

life's little, our heads
sad. Redeemed and wasting clay
this chance. Be of use.

The Tub (1886)

*Drawing is not what one sees but what one
can make others see.*
—*Edgar Degas*

The mirror on the wall disarms but the face
seen in a basin, scrubbed by hand to remove
the grime of surviving that sediments in streaks
is a truer reflection, not of what we might be
plumed & painted, but who we truly are when
every disguise drops away. *Femme de petite vertu,
fille en numéro et publique, soumise en maison,
raccrocheuse des boulevards*—names not a reason
to suggest the body's more than pliable parlor
meant to house some rich man's brief pleasure,
then be discarded, a filthy rag. Bone-weary,
bent over a tub, washing away a week's worth
of earning bread, sheer animus weighs enough
to drain this fallacy: a fugitive spool of water.

Sea Watchers (1952)

*I find in working, always the distracting
intrusion of elements not a part of my most
interested vision, and the inevitable obliteration
and replacement of this vision by the work
itself as it proceeds.*
—*Edward Hopper*

Not the Hamptons, even a half-century ago,
more barren in midday than a beach should be,
gull-less, garrulous only on the clothesline
where orange and yellow towels flutter dry.

Impassive as the angular stones in the sand,
husband and wife steep in the sun, silent.
It's been years since they felt any need
for small talk and now, childless, on vacation,

they've chosen a concrete shore house
to spend a week swimming, eating lobster
rolls at the shack in the center of town,
and watching the clear hyaline sea darken

in spots over the kelp-encrusted rocks.
At night, she will undress, carefully folding
her navy blue two-piece swimsuit over
the porcelain lip of the streaked claw-foot

tub that stands adjacent to the narrow bed
where he reclines, reading a *Popular Mechanics*.
She will unhook the clasp of the swim cap
under her chin to shake out her still damp

hair, to frown fractionally at the mirror
before getting into bed. In a few minutes,
he will place the magazine in the bedside
table's oak drawer, click off the lamp,

and without exchanging a word, hold her
by the ankles to better gain purchase
on the taut cotton sheets she will remake
in the morning when he jogs on the beach.

As Slow As Possible

If something is boring after two minutes, try it for four.
If still boring, then eight. Then thirty-two. Eventually
one discovers it is not boring at all.
—John Cage

Heard from a painter how the piece being performed
in a small church in Germany articulates to the history
of the organ, 639 years old in 2001 when the concert
began and scheduled to end in 2640, one note in years.
We were talking about duration in art, how we stop
on a word in a poem or stand in front of a painting
for thirty seconds that could easily be thirty minutes
or thirty years, but how music transpires in time
in a categorically different way, the sound departing
even as it arrives in our ear and nervous system.
This Cage piece is as close as someone could come
to freeing music from temporality, and it commenced
in St. Burchardi church in Halberstadt on what would
have been Cage's 89th birthday and because the score
begins on the rest, it started with a 17-month silence,
save for the sound of the bellows of the instrument
encased in acrylic glass being inflated. Every time
a note changes there's a party and at the last chord-
shift, which will last for 7 years, there were thousands
of visitors, international correspondents and camera
crews, an event broadcast worldwide on a website.
Hyperdurational, said the painter. Only in Germany.

Rodeo Cowboy No. 1 (1978)

Subject-matter is at best a vehicle to transcend
—Fritz Scholder

Giddy up pigment! Ride them blue horse!
In a dervish
                    of dust that disquiets
                            the limbs
hoof like a boot   spur on the flank
tail a trail   that recedes into green hills
        whole organism launched   in mid-air
without crowdnoise   without leatherburn
                    depth an occluded measurement
vertiginous   rider a totemic showman
                    back turned
                            faceless
                                    hint of a brim
day an overall yolk yellow flattened dimensionless
animal and man primal less the primacy of paint

Maine Islands (1938)

a gathering of words of other fondled words begotten is called
investigation, and this in turn is called cerebral rapture
—Mardsen Hartley

Rough edged wilderness, all crag, surf, pines & sky,
a land before the lobstermen, logging crews, iron works,

& Acadians had bent the natural shapes into commerce,
before the radiocarbon dated Red Paint People some say

according to medieval Rabbinic fables descended from one
of the lost tribes of Israel yet who gouged out mollusks

with flaked stone, hunted swordfish & buried their own
in graves of red ocher—*when the surf licks with its tongues*—

before the Paleo-Indians followed musk ox & caribou,
wooly mammoths & giant bison across the Bering Land

Bridge into Alaska & through a corridor between glaciers
leaving behind a trail of spear tips with fluted points,

but after the last glaciation had receded to leave turbulent
brush-strokes—*these volcanic personal shapes*—a flat plane

between foreground & background with no sign of human
presence—*which we defining for ourselves as rocks accept them*

as such—the horizon bathed blue when clouds shrink
above the serrated treeline & below the chunky, brown

& slate, grainy, Cezannesque earth—*its feverish incoming*—
a primitivist landscape, part physical presence deliberately

stitch-stroked onto canvas, part transcendent intermediary
between air & infinite space—*those restless entities disturbing*

solid substances—that emerges from the view that predates
sight, making the stubble of dried paint a mood of longing,

like the secret mourning of a man for his Nazi German
officer lover killed fighting on the front & never replaced

from the center of a restless, peripatetic existence in quest
of something purer—*a curious, irrelevant, common fret*—

where landscape's lack of depth has its own depthlessness
& the sea like the past recedes & approaches, palpitates,

a place like Vinalhaven, Isle au Haut, Mantinicus, Hupper
& off into the Cisco Bay. A place starker & more isolated

than now, dangerous—*the inwash cooling at least the eye*—
yet lyric in its childlike grandeur hung to see in a frame.

Movements

Dance is an art in space and time.
The object of the dancer is to obliterate that.
—Merce Cunningham

What an endeavor, nine of you
touring in a VW van, bringing new forms
            of elasticity into being on stages where the crowd,
    if they came at all, would not stay long
                enough to realise they were witness to history
in the dancing, conjunctions
            of chance in music, sets, steps the likes of which
                    had never before been choreographed—
    Hip jut, asynchronous strut, feline pounce,
                convulsive pirouette, collapses,
        the appearance of notes on a prepared piano
                giving way to silence that was really the sound
of moving feet: women flowing continuously,
        men in spurts, around, together, apart,
                    together, in between, over, around,
        with calves stretched, torsos contorted,
                wrists flung out from behind ears like freestyle
swimmers squeezing every last ounce
                of speed from their long strokes,
                        not telling a story,
        but articulating each movement in full
                before falling away, rising into the next instant,
    not knowing beforehand how it might feel
                to respond to the music,
        revealing that in costume, on stage, in motion,
                bodies need embody nobody
                        save beauty.

The Day the Voice Died (1998)

If you possess something but can't give it away, then you
don't possess it ... it possesses you.
—*Frank Sinatra*

—after Frank O'Hara

It is nearly 1:50 in New York a Thursday
Dante Alighieri and George Lucas' birthday,
anniversary of the day Jamestown was settled,
yes and it is not last call, not in the self-
proclaimed center of the world where the gas
is poured till the slivery moon is closer to light
than dark and I'm boxed in by finks who think
they're big-leaguers when the game's wiffle-ball,
pawing their cell phones and high-fiving,
and wouldn't it have been perfect if Blue Eyes
came on the jukebox and a busload of bobbysoxers
poured in, but no, this is real life, 1998
                    and I'm holding
a watered down vodka tonic in a haze of smoke,
and there're no screws wearing suits with fabric
finer in the lining than upon slim lapels, no crooning,
no louche swagger or clacking of billiard balls,
hardly no one carrying a Zippo and a roll of dimes,
and I will finish my drink, walk down the Avenue
of the Americas to the A/C/E line running local,
moving slower than I should, in synchronicity
with cabs idling curbside and across the Hudson,
Hoboken, which I can't see, glittering languidly,
one might even say, except for this fact of real life,
in a pose of mourning, pouring wave after wave
of brass and bel canto from here to eternity.

In Spanish, the Toreador's Outfit is Called
a Suit of Lights

Everything alters me, but nothing changes me.
—Salvador Dalí

From Maximo to Sterling Manor, down Clam Bayou to Coquina Key,
St. Pete's once had a world record 768 straight days of illumination.

Sunshine City. As florid & fantastic a place as any to celebrate
Salvador Dalí who claimed not to do drugs, because he was drugs.

There among palm fronds waving at a more distant, bobbing forest
of masts, a wormlike blob composed of over a thousand different

faceted triangular pieces of glass engulfs the vertices of the hurricane-
proof minimalist box that houses the rest of the art. Like being inside

a giant fly's eye, this free-form geodesic bubble, a liquid gesture
to amassing clouds, nearly translucent, shimmers to eat the rational

concrete walls. Its creator, an architect who previously worked
with I.M. Pei on the Louvre's glass pyramid calls it 'the enigma'.

Appropriate for the famous moustache about whom André Breton
coined the anagrammatic nickname 'Avida Dollars', the seeker

who flummoxed Mike Wallace with his discovery of 'the logarithmic
curve of cauliflower' & 'the erotics of everything', the superstitious

Spaniard with a pet ocelot named Babou on leash & collar, the would-be
Moor cultivating 'creative paranoia' with Gala by his side,

the nuclear mystic collaborating with Alfred Hitchcock on *Spellbound*,
the childhood bat-eater visiting Sigmund Freud in London,

nearly asphyxiating himself in a deep-sea diving suit, casting Alice
Cooper as a hologram, always just a false eyelash or two beyond

grossly excessive in his life, his art. Now I'm striding past real rocks
meant to be simulacra of formations from his native Cadaqués,

the biomorphic ones that jut & hang in many of his dreamscapes,
those childhood crags, cuneiforms replete with rock pools

where he once scripted *Un Chien Andalou* with Luis Buñuel.
Now having streamed through a box-hedge spotted grotto, an avant-

garden laid out according to the proportions of the golden rectangle,
I'm shimming up the helical staircase, modeled on the molecular

strand, to stand confronting the monumental *The Hallucinogenic Toreador*
whose Venus is as close to goddess as I have come since gazing

upon *Notre Dame de la Belle Verrière*, the intricate blue-hued, stained
glass Virgin at Chartres. This Venus de Milo is a double image glimpsed

from the logo on a mass produced color pencil case that onionskinned
into other faces in shadow in Dali's mind, a doleful bullfighter

draped in the Spanish colors, tiny dots turning into St. Narciso flies
in squadron formation forming his cap & cape, a bull whose glassy-eyed

decapitated head pools in blood, no, it's a translucent bay, a raft
not on coagulating but wavering water at the foot of the Cliffs

of Creus, the whole protean spectacle contained in a Palladian arena
where amid floating roses, a bust of Voltaire, flecks of reflecting

colour resolving into a Dalmatian, this statue from antiquity
embodying feminine beauty reduplicates ad infinitum, growing

more archetypal & less precise in the distance, stretching back
through time as in those dated depictions of evolutionary progress

where the hunched simian finally straightens into a naked white man.
Dalí received her as a gift in his youth & our Venus changes shapes

& gender, her immortal breast really the toreador's nose,
her green skirt his tie, beatified Gala looking down disapprovingly

from one edge while from the other, dressed in a sailor suit,
holding a hoop & a fossilised bone, the artist's child self, half-turned

away from us to watch the swarm: flies, atoms, breasts, dreams.
All we see & missee evolving from & returning to a common ancestor.

Funk & Wag: Revivals to Schopenhauer (2012)

The survival of my own ideas may not be as important as a condition I might create for others' ideas to be realized.
—*Mel Chin*

1.

Play that Romulus like a ring-billed gull sculls	= play
for fish, focused, plucking those she-wolf teats	= fish
like saxophone keys until the Sabine women,	= like
seized, bleat & drag their bare feet for pleasure	= pleasure
that resembles terror the closer they come,	= terror
the closer they come. Resignation, roundheads,	= resignation
is Schopenhauer's supreme wisdom, all impulse,	= wisdom
pulse & palsy, *rouge et noir* played until *refait*,	= until
until Saturn's rings are rung with Ramses' ring	= rings
& the finger candy of a Frankish king a beaver	= Finger
will pilfer to weave his dream dam like a prayer	= prayer
rug trimmed with tread like a block of rubber	= tread
sliced for tire stock, another polymer vulcanised	= another
for profit. Cut & paste to accrue & negate context.	= negate
Channel the indefinite multiplicity of the material	= indefinite
& immaterial world for to stand still is to petrify.	= still
Even words veer across the page trailing a dust	= words
tail of histories that hide in interstices between	= hide
letters. From Rochester to Saratov, Saarbrücken	= letters
to Santiago, Rome to Ruanda-Urundi or Saipan	= to
to Rhodesia, the great books necessarily dissemble.	= books
Rather present a partial perspective that torn out	= perspective
& reimagined can be seen again, gathered in form,	= form
modulated to order, placed & reconfigured, shaped	= to
to less provincial taxonomy through the processes	= through
of sanitary engineering, fused into hybrids of life.	= fused

Juxtapose, then, flow of space over time until new   = new
performances, which while familiar resemble nothing   = nothing
ever before experienced, can occur: a collective self-   = self
portrait with flags & machines; a miscegenation   = portrait
of bird & insect fashioning an illegible glyph;   = illegible
a rabbit with ribcage antlers for ears; a garland   = with
of icons of unknown origin; cracked, androgynous   = unknown
busts basted back together so gender is rendered   = rendered
archaic; renowned mouths of mouthpieces muted   = muted
into a frozen wave a single sailboat like a rock   = wave
sits silently upon; a bridge traversing dimensions   = dimensions
of wealth from arid tableland to azure coast;   = arid
natives at the well & man as the root of the tree.   = the
Cue up the zany *vidushakas* to slapstick & parody   = cue
the royal court with thick makeup, simian beards   = the
& Sanskrit barbs. Sprinkle in a few schnausers   = barbs
snacking on shit-dwelling scarab beetles & shade   = shade
the silky salukis with sails so they can't see or smell   = the
the noxious cloverleaves exploding the sacred   = exploding
into a storm of shrapnel that once fragmented   = shrapnel
will forever remain in fragments: continents adrift   = forever
in rising water, shards of phenomenon arising   = shards
from the universal will's irrational, embryological   = irrational
energy where the body is an idea & the punchline   = body
of the cosmic joke is simply that God is a gun.   = the

2.

The body, irrational, shards forever.   = forever
Shrapnel exploding the shade barbs   = exploding
the cue. The arid dimensions wave,   = dimensions
muted, rendered unknown with illegible   = unknown
portrait. Self nothing new, fused through   = new
to form perspective. Books to letters hide   = form
words still indefinite, negate another tread   = words
prayer. Finger rings until wisdom,   = until
resignation, terror, pleasure, like fish play.   = play

3.

Play until words form new unknown dimensions exploding forever.

A Square of Blue Infinity

The true adventurer goes forth aimless
and uncalculating to meet and greet
unknown fate.
—O. Henry

Snookered by traffic lights that turn
the swim up 9 into a knot,
Middletown's fringe tediously damp
with the same almost-wet that streaks

the windshields in such a way
that wipers twitch ineffectively
against the hard light, clear edges,
what Pound claimed no democratised

campaign could maintain stages
its revival upon the smudged glass.
morning. Red stutter of brakelights.
Wide world winnowed to a stretch

of road from the coast to Hartford,
my passage sealed from traffic
and saturated with felicitous diction,
the glories of books on tape,

dear sir, your stories spoken by
a second-rate thespian for whom
even commercials have dried up.
Nearly a century since you hopped

a freighter into the banana boom,
wanted by the feds for bank fraud,
just another *gringo* in Honduras
with a scar the source of which

he'd rather not reveal over mojitos.
did prison teach you the difference
between prosaic and prosodic
prose or was it being feted

in the streets of the city you died in as
'Caliph of Bhagdad-by-the-Subway',
most colourful newspaperman in the five
boroughs? You'd work all winter

on fifths of scotch while editors
screamed for copy, putting down
the occasional yarn on a typewriter
missing a few keys. You outwitted it

by using a period for an apostrophe.
Somewhere pent in your small flat,
hunched over an overflowing ashtray,
memories of endless, rolling Prairie

must have uncharted the city's grid,
leaving you a brief glimpse
into something so large that no one
could ever belong to or even trace

its terrible shape, though you tried
with sinuously wound sentences
laden with polysyllables, brogue,
and what became a characteristic

plot twist. I've heard your critics
complain that you're too mannered,
your phraseology ostentatious,
your enduring reputation as a hack,

but what art rebuffs contrivance?
Even the trees flaming into autumn
north of Middletown *look* different
to each of the passing drivers

and *are* something altogether other,
like your stately delineations
that run from the 'hectic, haggard
perfunctory welcome like the specious

smile of a demirep' to 'a polychromatic
rug like some brilliant-flowered,
rectangular, tropical islet surrounded
by a billowy sea of soiled matting',

all in the course of the same story,
one that is not believable, true,
but not meant to be, any more
than Sophocles intended Oedipus

Rex to be a literal transcription
of a typical Athenian nobleman's
quirky yet predestined misfortune.
No, you are like the conductor

of a Viennese waltz, peering
past your gloves as the orchestra
swells, as a gentleman in tails
bows low above his lady's hand,

lips poised above but never making
contact with her niveous flesh,
proving that between a thought
and its realisation, space is infinite.

In your world, the wrong man
gets the right job, bums who want
to be arrested can't, while rich
misers receive sudden comeuppance.

you and I both know it's akin
to dance, not cartography,
analogy, not mimetic affirmation,
that the trajectory of no life

could so gracefully arc towards
a spindle of fate, abruptly changing
direction. Unless of course we take
yours: frail North Carolina

ex-con who rose to international
literary renown in less than nine years,
then died in a New York hospital,
penniless, drunk, and alone, uttering

last words that one of his own
characters might have spoken:
'Turn up the lights, I don't want
to go home in the dark'.

From where I'm sitting,
there is no dark, the whole sky
is lit up like a stadium, a thick braid
of traffic forms then unravels,

the Cisco Kid has just traversed
an arroyo to find his cheating lover,
and next to me a gaunt woman mouths
lyrics, slowly, to a song I cannot hear.

Pataphysics

It is extremely difficult to stay alert & attentive
instead of getting hypnotized by the constant
monologue inside your head.

— David Foster Wallace

How the Search Ended

Before the bus flattened me,
I was searching for a scent
never to be remembered
until it was smelled again.

My fault not the driver's:
I had stopped to stare at a girl
undressing in her window.
I was too far to smell her.

Earlier, I had visited a palm reader,
not to trace my lifeline, merely
to discover where to buy
an oversized neon hand.

On the way home, my head jangled
with a premise: Life is either more or less
serious than I imagine it to be.
and then came the bus.

Conjoined

I have come to love you in spite of
—Darin Strauss, Chang and Eng

straddling the windowsill
from the terminal   spectral gray
cools   here near where
hosing down cleft sidewalks
loops of barbed wire that gem
of caffeine beginning to rotate
to feel nose hairs filtering breath
this early   filled still with dawn
unfastening shutters   one pulse
resolves the screen into a voice

watching morning glimmer
becoming blonde as coffee
chirrups erupt   whoosh of man
raising wraiths of spray against
in early sun   invisible spokes
into awareness   porous enough
the closest to psalms I come
tuning strings   swooping pigeons
in pure influence until the remote
that fills the room like cologne

*…stigmatised for years as circus
spectacles, hear what it's really like
to be connected to a sibling…*

conjoined twins flash
craniums   one faces
sheen of polished teeth
grinning beneath a solid side

on screen   two girls kissing
one way   the other   another
their specialist doctor
shield mask to address us

*…the result of a rare embryological
accident has made these two
sisters literally inseparable …*

'serenity now' stops working
tissue   they can't be split
who speaks at what time
the bathroom   only agreeing
slightly torments them

contracts   sharing brain
must negotiate where to go
how to dress   when to use
being out in public
suddenly   I love them more

for that 'slightly'
from *spina bifida*   still hopes
the other wants to be a nurse
they turn a practiced orbit
chance to address the camera

one a minute older   suffers
to become a country singer
both hope to be mothers
each allowing the other equal
looking directly through me

...I can't imagine life without her
yet every day I try. I think God made us
this way because we are special...

then the keyboard synth loop
blind sunrise blithely persistent
I don't even know their names
holy land rather on synapses
signals of spectrum parabola-shot
the same amount of time

pounds their faces to commercial
flickering through the window
try to recall hope   to feel whole
gray matter   invisible ubiquitous
antenna-caught every single second
4.2 babies take to be born

The Three Christs

Waiting for the Norwegian poet to read
her poems, you delineated the differences
between you and her by pointing to Jesus.

Her version, you said, was radiating outwards,
wave and astral particle, revelatory energy
and blinding light, inherently metaphysical.

Your version, however, was dusty and dog-
tired, having walked too long too far in feet
that ached, in draggled robes, in desperate

need of a hot bath, bread, a goblet of wine,
something to take his mind off those carping
apostles, those omnipresent Roman soldiers.

Sitting here, alone, looking out at the play
of sun and shadow on crenellated ferns,
I'm conjuring a third Christ, neither weary

nor luminous, but one who lives nowhere
save within me, indwelling life illimitable
that I will remain estranged from so long

as I insist on insisting, on putting my own
pleasure, which is all I know deeply or well,
first. A Christ who wears my body's garment.

Raise the stone, there thou shalt find me;
cleave the wood and there I am. Let not
him who seeks cease until he finds. When

he finds, he shall be astonished. Astonished,
he shall reach the Kingdom. Having reached
the Kingdom, he shall (shall he? shall I?) rest.

One Stone to Samadhi

Back in the room, it's as if we never left:
a cone of frangipani gradually charring,
and *Clair de Lune*, overlaid with whale song,

piping through tweeters in the background,
plastic folding-chairs filled with disparate frames
in similar postures: back straight, palms open

upon thighs, eyes closed, muscles relaxed,
the flicker of thought, in principle, sacrificed
to the rising and falling of breath. Still a fleck

of peripheral self can't help but remain, temporarily
unhooked from memory's flux and grapple,
yet attendant in some form nonetheless,

a watchfulness impartial to inclination,
though to speak of it is like pointing a finger
at the moon. Suffice it to say that, eyes closed,

the crest on passing time's ongoing wave
perpetually furnishes the mind with vista,
and back in the room, it's as if we never arrived.

Symbiosis

One alternative to speech is wheatless streets
where caught mid-impetus, even lampposts
rusted cursive partake of flow:
this into that, shadow ceding mass, intake output,
not headed anywhere particularly but particular
nonetheless, the way the cracked curb
appears granular in sunlight,
both existing not from their own end
but in symphony with that which converts
their presence into nouns, as if that fixes
anything in place, root-sure with the necessity
of clavicles, igneous rocks and thunderclaps.
with obstinate grace things slip name's knots.
a bright moth, lanced on pins of rhetoric,
sloughs off tremulous meaning, even in decay,
even under the magnifying glass' oblong eye.
only a blossom can define proboscis.

Primitives

Banish the glaze of objects from the firmament,
undu formica and fundament, pinch off the ridges
of the Caucasus, andirons of clay used in hearths
some four millennia ago. Ask how blind urges
creolised in burnished arabesque surfaces
that once glowed in fire are now backlit in humidity-
controlled glass capsules indexed by number,
defined by placard, sold at auction. Recall
that clusters of bird bones found buried with relics
are those of *Gallus gallus*—the domestic chicken.
Trace a chain of Y-chromosomes from the Upper
Paleolithic imagination to rock walls scarred
with petroglyphs and handprints. To poems.
Burnish the gaze of subjects with firm remnants.

Instrumentality

For true *handschumachers*, whose numbers, thanks to machines,
have dwindled, stitching together gloves is the highest calling.

Preferable to shearing bolts of cloth or shoeing in a tatty alley,
as the old joke goes, whoever saw anyone speak using their boots?

Glove-making is true art and hierarchical in profession as five
Fingers: silkers, closers, fourchetters, all under the thumb of cutters

who can tell at a glance whether a cut of leather is South African
capeskin or peccary shorn from Brazilian wild boars, whether a glove

is sewn with half- or full-piqué stitches, its finish velvet or grain.
Such depths of knowing exist in the performance of any occupation

from learning how to hold a rattan and rubber marimba mallet
to memorising the occult order of four cylinders and sixteen valves.

Even communication is apprenticeship in hue and nuance,
contains garlands of articulated sound to festoon upon toolcraft:

praise the intervention of utensils for extending person into matter!
Praise the crows, levers, handspikes, pinions, cranks, winches,

cams, pedals, wedges, screws, heddles, wheels, planes, springs,
latches, keys that provide attention a momentary respite from itself,

because in fleeting occupation, even the most dogged ego dissolves.
The diffusion of personality via tools is grace, so grace to the fingers

of the pastry chef who kneads dough into flour and grace to the flags
the air-traffic controller whisks through the runway's turbulent air,

grace for all task which focuses notice to the eviction of doubt,
leaving action's unstuttering arc, which is eloquence and muteness

at once, to turn the bars of time into a provisional, shoreless field.
I want to live where glove-makers are singular artificers in the world

in which their pliers ply. I'll swap you my head for a stabbing awl.
Remember when the first basalt flakes were chipped from boulders

to make hand-axes that could dismember most carcasses the hominid
we once were might have hunted down? The moment when the words

sunder and *salmonella* entered the language? Was it corporeal act
before idea, disembodied before uttered as sound? Did the Triangulum

have a pinwheel before we a telescope? That's a koan, unanswerable—
better to lay eyeglasses at Hephaestus' forge as alms for the prosthetics

which grant our bodies metaphors for itself. Because before the invention
of the pump, there was one less way to understand the human heart.

Blotched in Transmission

Bark of the birch, aria of the oriole, grit of the sand-grain,
in the first stanza I shall attempt to confiscate your essence
and each time, you will slip through the noose of language,
having no owner. Your brief appearance, though, is enough
for the covetous page, conferring the illusion of presence.

Even the breaths heaving in my chest do not belong to me,
these wires of muscles tapping the hand's opposable thumb
upon the spacebar, and the precise machinery of two pupils
taking it in are not mine, though convenient to think so.
In the second stanza, I shall feel like an outsider in my body.

Emptied of the need to own, I become the pit of a plum.
We color our language, Wallace Stevens wrote to Elsie Moll,
and Truth, being white, becomes blotched in transmission.
In the third, final stanza, I will understand what he meant
for a moment, before the old words come flooding back.

Spangling the Sea

Ruffle and tuck, river fabric wags doggedly towards ocean,
heaping surface on surface, its cadence a gown.

Perpetually beneath lurks stillness, a calm inseam sewn
by handless needles, distinct from yet part of the sequined

design that glints iridescent now, then dark as pine.
between silt and waver live many denizens of the deep:

zigzagging shiners, freshwater drums, tessellated darters,
grass carp, a kaleidoscopic plenitude that yaws and rolls

among root wads and bubble curtains drawn on riparian
terraces, hinged vertebrae whipping back and forth

in an elastic continuum displacing the fluid milieu,
enabling them, polarised or not, to scull along in schools.

Nothing in outer space so bizarre as episodes underwater:
the gilled emerge from bouts of massive oviparity

staged upon plankton columns where some fry turn larval
while the majority never leave the sure rot of egg sleep.

Whether due to snowmelt in mountainous headwater tracts
or to rainfall from cumulonimbus fancy, for whatever reason

water appears from serpentine soil and prairie-scrub mosaic,
a small muddy trickle that gains momentum as it swells

and deepens, sweeping along twigs, carcasses, bald tires,
to empty at length into estuaries engulfed by tides

perpetually born of a body dressed in hastening garb,
upholstering two-thirds more surface than any ground.

Fabricating Astrology

I lie on my back in the damp grass,
staring at the stars' mineral precision.
Masses of gas, bearers of dead light,
mysteries snared by unreachable lairs,

how many pairs of eyes have swilled
from your glass and grown thirstier?
Will our progeny decode your songs?
My heart gives its usual answer: thrum.

The longer I gape, the more the many
nebulae appear latticed, like a screen
in windows or a page of graph paper,
ordered as the placement of fibulas

in feet. The chart seems plotted
along three axes: love, labor, time.
besotted hours converge into minus,
kind and curative movements belong

to plus, and mirrored, both data-sets
verge towards an identical asymptote,
death, provider of cardinal boundary,
maker of the silence shapes merge with

eventually. This much is certain:
Today I'm a day closer to extinction.
Hearse-curtains have been drawn
in every city while the stars remain

anchored overhead. Really they move
towards annulment in a proof i cannot
prove. Soon enough, pattern dissolves.
Let me replace them with these words.

Plumbing the Deepening Groove

That survival is impossible without repetition
of patterns is platitude—see moon rise or whorls in wolf fur—

but how explain the human need to reenact primal dramas,
even when the act perpetuates a cycle of abuse?

The boy who hides in the tool shed with buckle-shaped welts
rising like figs from his arms will curse his father,

and in turn beat his son. Like a wave anguish rises,
never understands itself before emptying in a fist.

The spurned daughter will seek out lovers who abandon her,
self-will degenerating in the face of what feels familiar.

Childhood, seen in light of recurrence, takes on the heft
of conspiracy, casts a shadow across an entire life,

making it appear that nothing could have happened
differently, that free and easy is the stuff of semblance.

Then of the prerogatives, reclamation is principal,
to appraise the past the way a painter subsumes old canvas

with new layers of paint, each brushstroke unconcerned,
sure, dismantling the contour of what once was realised

so that new forms can emerge to contradict the suggestion
that survival is impossible without repetition.

Language Poetry

Language poem for Leslie Scalapino

Yea, it was pundit debunking, sage with newness,
meaty ruse, elaborate masquerade of unmeaning,

stage where words pose counterpoised to signification,
where rummy syllables string along kinks of syntax

and gum of virgules jimmies together clauses
to devise a monument of fistulous happenstance,

subverting address for free play—
Rare vestiges pitched headlong in stochastic

eddies, dreaming a livelong laterality,
polygons alongside tapirs in grammar-shorn dance—

Slithered mid-speech an intention a seam
the color of politics, even the furthest minutia

run on dollars, come what cannot until (s)pace
Breaks into half itself &

music the bramble where bare verbs rabble,
seeking the iota behind the bestial bars

that proves no forged lattice girds the mind
with predicates efficacious as prison searchlights—

Senses slip the faster usurps fate from syntax
how kowtow to solipsism or preset a page?

Pyramid Starship

In the end the afrofuturists have it right—
Time to move on, Funkadelic, light years
in time so far ahead of our time that tight-
weaves braid a distant, blacker dimension
of which crystal headdresses, silver Dashikis,
& a fur-rimmed amulet spinning eye of Horus,
are gateways to another world.

                    Pontos riscados,
chalked cosmograms, sigils used in ritual
to invoke the Orixas and stave off the fears
of an immolating whiteness way too much
mayonnaise slathered on bone white bread.
Make your own music. Just don't bore us,
from apex to base beams the flying saucer:
I am on this planet because people need me.

Notes towards Timekeeping

Interrogate the role of the clock in the maintenance of Empire.

Take the 1884 Prime Meridian Conference. The 'universal' hour, Greenwich Mean, favoured industry to agriculture, punching in to the peripatetic, plugged and debugged to poaching like an egg in a brass kettle.

Nothing nearer yet more far than fin-de-siècle.

Spaces gravid with teleological forms. Silences and elisions. Swathes of season that know no secondhand. Attempts to articulate sanitised versions of nomadic culture in corporeal form fail. Perfected bodies strapped to the wrist are subtle acts of terrorism.

Compare means of measurement:

> Scratch marks on bones or sticks made with a stone. Count the interval between phases of the moon, or like the Egyptians watch for the Dog Star to rise more or less when the inundation of the Nile begins.

> Or shift grains in an hourglass: powdered eggshell, marble dust or sand to pass through a channel ten times the size of any single particle.

> Else verge escapement. Floating clepsydra. The astrolabe a devil's star-grasper.

> Remember pizoelectric quartz over time, due to temperature change, impurity, or decay, will lose its accuracy, drift, misquote the hour.

If a clock reading half past one on a railway car hurtling through New London at sixty-six miles per hour crosses the path of a robin migrating south for the winter by pausing on every twentieth telephone pole for an average of forty-eight seconds, what time is it in the mind of the knock-kneed Indian boy who waits for the light to change so he can check the comic book store to see if the new issue of the Watchmen, which he will read while his parents quarrel about his future, is currently on the rack.

Anything with moving hands both disables and enables a spectatorial position that cannot be graphed on axes.

'The essence of nowness runs
like fire along the fuse of time.'
—George Santayana

Like a marigold feeling elongates into an outer fringe pulled taut as a shawl over the eyes or crouching inside a shrub where footfall has been grown over green and withered to appear again, briefly luminescent, not yours but more you than your own embodiment, though all desire to possess it vanishes, since some desires reside in a stillness where motion ceases and where you begin with tentative strokes to recollect what in retrospect cannot be recreated, what was in fact and will remain without semblance, what could not be, but nonetheless right now, is.

Drip-drop a precursor to tick-tock a precursor to beep-beep-beep.

On the Spanish slave schooner, the Amistad, the ship's passengers, snatched from Sierra Leone, revolted, sparing only the navigator his sextant, but instead of being returned home, ended up being seized by the United States Navy, interred in a New Haven jail, argued over by abolitionists and federal courts and marked Cuban merchandise by the Spanish, until, a few years later, accompanied by Christian missionaries, they were returned to their village. How would you quantify the passage of time for them contrasted with the lives of those who had been left in West Africa?
'Time is fulfilled when time is no more.
He who in time has his heart established
in eternity and in whom all temporal things

are dead, in him is the fullness of time.'
—Meister Eckhart.

Well into the Sung dynasty, the Chinese calibrated sticks of incense to measure time, using different scents at different intervals, so that hours became shifting fragrances. Sandalwood sunrises, jasmine at noon, juniper evenings, myrrh presaging dusk, the threads unraveling and dropping into a sounding plate, the air charged with notes to read in the nose.

Dram is to scruple is to grain is to fraction of a gram is to measurable duration.

Noon in New York	7:00 PM, Cape Town, South Africa
La Paz, Bolivia	8:00 PM in Baghdad, Iraq
2:00 PM, Rio de Janeiro, Brazil	10:30 PM in Bombay, India
5:00 PM, Casablanca, Morocco	Midnight in Bangkok, Thailand
4:00 PM, Reykjavik, Iceland	1:00 AM, next day, Shanghai, China
6:00 PM, Oslo, Norway	3:00 AM, next day Melbourne, Australia

Standardisation is to make uniform. Uniforms when worn show coherence. Allow for identification and lack of variation, diversity or change in degree. Standardisation and uniforms go hand in hand. Uniforms and force go hand in hand. During the holiday season, this can take the shape of travel alarm clocks and page-a-day calendars.

When you are young, a wizened man in a dhoti said to me once on the dusty road to the fruit bazaar, you think in hours. Your next birthday is forever away, driving a car unthinkable. When you are older, you think in years. The year you finished school, the year you met your wife, the year the floods washed away the rice paddies. When you are older yet, you think in decades. My twenties were such a free and confusing time. In my forties, life finally started to make sense. When you are my age, he said, fixing me with a steely eye, peeling a hank of sugarcane with his few remaining front teeth, you think again in moments. Now is all you have. Now. And now. And eternity.

> 'Because time is out there, eaten by light.'
> —Norma Cole.

Time out. You got the time? Make time for me. Save time by cutting in line. How did you spend your time? Time is cash. He was gone a long time. I'll tell you about it some other time. Once upon time, time stood still. From that time on, nothing was ever the same. Now there's never enough time. It's an inopportune time. Time out of joint. Untimely. Like a ticking time bomb. But once you've served hard time. Taken it one day at a time. Time and time again. Can't make up that time. Not in our time.

Wait for nothing, for nothing will come to pass.

In the movies, time is abetted by edits. Cut from a plane taking off to a plane landing in the same airport. A voyage taken place, time has passed. Cut from a zoom in of a door handle to the interior of a room: space has been moved through, fast forward ahead. Use a montage of images to depict passing time; use voiceover to move the action forwards, backwards, into and away from the leading edge of the narrative. Cinematic time, save the hours in the theater, is the elaborate construction of fiction.

Or take the projectionist in his dark booth, running a reel backwards, so the coffee flows back into the pot, the butter smoothes off the toast, the sizzling eggs liquefy then leap from the pan back into their eggshells.

Because between any two instants, there is a third, and between them, another and another, an unquantifiable infinity of them, strung along a linear continuum like shrinking beads on an invisible string.

> Time is a form of becoming.
> Form the time of becoming.
> Becoming the form of time.

Singularities

It is singularity which often makes the worst part
of our suffering, as it always does of our conduct.

—Jane Austen

Exile

There's nowhere else I'd rather not be than here,
but here I am nonetheless, *dispossessed,*
though not quite, because I never owned
what's been taken from me, never have belonged
in and to a place, a people, a common history.
Even as a child when I was slurred in school—
towel head, dot boy, camel jockey—
none of the abuse was precise: only Sikhs
wear turbans, widows and young girls *bindus,*
not one species of camel is indigenous to India…
If, as Simone Weil writes, to be rooted
is the most important and least recognised need
of the human soul, behold: I am an epiphyte.
I conjure sustenance from thin air and the smell
of both camphor and meatloaf equally repel me.
I've worn a *lungi* pulled between my legs,
done designer drugs while subwoofers throbbed,
sipped *masala chai* steaming from a tin cup,
driven a Dodge across the Verrazano in rush hour,
and always to some degree felt extraneous,
like a meteorite happened upon bingo night.
This alien feeling, honed in aloneness to an edge,
uses me to carve an appropriate mask each morning.
I'm still unsure what effect it has on my soul.

Contraction

Honest self-scrutiny too easily mutinies,
        mutates into false memories
which find language a receptive host,
boosted by boastful embellishments.

Self-esteem is raised on wobbly beams,
        seeming seen as stuff enough
to fund the hedge of personality,
though personally, I cannot forget

whom I have met and somehow wronged,
        wrung for a jot of fugitive juice,
trading some ruse for a blot or two,
labored to braid from transparent diction

fiction, quick fix, quixotic fixation.
        As the pulse of impulses
drained through my veins, I tried to live
twenty lives at once. Now one is plenty.

Immediate Family

Homonymic sonnet for Rajee Shankar

1)   Though it might not have been readily apparent,
         I saw my father, ever conscious of dollars & cents,
         filch toilet paper from a maid's cart. Not a parent-
         like thing to do, granted, nothing that makes sense
         given his comportment. I wonder if he could choose
         differently or if he was just acting in a waking daze,
         a kleptomaniac stupor. Watching the way he chews
         his food sometimes, I puzzle what pleasure his days
         on earth might consist of & how I might be his son
         when his default mode of looking is to glare. Pried
         open, what dreams might orbit his heart as the sun
         harnesses planets to spin? All I see his dark pride.
         This stranger, my father, a Tamilian of Brahmin caste,
         remains elusive no matter how many lines I cast.

2)   Finding out she was betrothed, my mother bawled
         in the high branch of a banyan tree, uncertain whether
         to jump or to hide knowing she was to marry the bald
         man come to marry her sister but in the shifting weather
         of Vedic astrological charts, much better suited to hold
         her hand. She was 19, he 30 & they had yet to meet.
         That long first afternoon, she preferred to stay holed
         up until her father called to say the man ate no meat,
         was kind & came from a good family. God who knows
         best would want nothing more for her. So down the limb
         she shimmied, wiping away tears & her ringed nose
         on the sleeve of her salwar kameez. She was yet to limn
         the shape of her life to be in America, frying bread
         not from lentil batter. For that, she was not yet bred.

3)   In Hindu myth, Yama, God of death, is no mere idol
but incarnation of justice, dharma, who will plumb
the deeds of a mortal life. Astride a buffalo, never idle,
holding mace and noose, dark as a rotting green plum,
he decides each next life in accordance with what's fair.
As a teenager, I would sit in temple under an ornate frieze
of gods, trying my hardest not to estimate the airfare
it took to bring these sculptures to the winter freeze
of Virginia from Southern India, my stomach in a knot
while old Sanskrit slokas, rich with meanings I missed
completely droned on. What's just? Shame? Why me, not
you, stuck with smelly barefoot Indians? Then from mist,
I saw a shape: myself looking back at me without lesson
or reprieve in lucent outlines that have yet to lessen.

Sam the Super

Villanelle for K.H. Shankar

You wouldn't take my bald father for a quirky man,
since his bearing is quintessentially Tamil-Brahmin,
a *Tam-Bram* for the uninitiated, with the firmest hand

when it comes to discipline or studies. He leers at ham
and beer alike. Believes what genes conspire within
him makes him purer than you. Not the sort of man

you'd ever imagine would in top hat willingly stand
in a Chinese restaurant smelling of wet dog and Ramen
to pull silk scarves from his mouth with his own hand,

yet there he was, amazingly, like Borat in Kazakhstan
but without the parody and much to my young chagrin,
playing the part of Magician, much more than mere man.

I was his caped and turbaned assistant who he'd demand
tap on boxes, say magical phrases, hide in a flour bin
he'd saw in half. If not a spectacle witnessed firsthand,

I wouldn't believe it either. Soon as he'd pull out a cyan
hanky to mop his brow in the parking lot, his large grin
would fade to a frown. He'd warn me not to say 'man'
or 'dude'. When I resisted, he pulled me to car by hand.

Stillness

Before the advent of expectation
        lives emptiness: distant hills blushing
                with the horizon, one B-flat pulled
                        apart at song's end,
      a hush of atoms holding together a planet. Father,

beyond plotting degree days, derivatives,
        sums and quotients, there is vacuum,
                a certainty that we are a conductor,
                        not *the* conductor,
      for a whole far greater than its parts. Amazing

relinquishing control. not the path
        of least resistance, not *a* path,
                but standing still as the sun drifts west,
                        as silence shorelines
      music, as hollow particles assert hallowed architecture.

In Illinois

for Sonya Sklaroff

The way was through the lawns and past the purr
of luxury sedans turning into
driveways gated by electronic eyes

and marble beasts. You spoke of how light steals
away each dawn which compels the brush
to sweep hue across the canvas, not to distill

the moment's sky—it has already forgotten
how to look—but rather, to satisfy
some twinge, the reason why you wake

at five each morning to paint. Overhearing
two mothers debate the merits of cash-
mere versus the pragmatism of wool,

we concluded that these suburbs were so safe
they were lethal. And then conversation
stopped; looming into the fog, without

an ocean's roar or salty slap, and down
a forested precipice was lake michigan:
vast, imbued and unfathomable.

Explosions Can Be Regenerative

for Gerry LeFemina

When the old coliseum where the Nighthawks used to play
fell precisely inwards on itself in a cloud of dust to the roar
of crowds watching on rooftops in their pajamas, for it was
early, I was headed to Union Station to catch Metro North
to the city. Better than fireworks, quipped the traffic guy
on the radio. What's better than seeing something smash?

It's true once I fell asleep on the red line, my face smashed
against one of the plastic seats, booze the hero of the play
that my liver, heart and head also starred in. Lucky some guy
didn't rifle through my pockets or write on me. No subway roar,
or even the addled rants of a man wearing an Ollie North
pin and distributing pamphlets on how the Holy Ghost was

friendlier than Casper, could disturb me then. Not when I was
drooling, no joke, and missed my Brooklyn stop smashed
into sleep and only roused agog in the Bronx, South to North.
Slept and again woke in the Bronx, like in an absurdist play
where time was recurrent and distant sea's muffled roar
replaced any dialogue. Scary. I was a wild and crazy guy

back then, would crash art openings featuring any guy
catering chardonnay to accompany his charcoals. My motto was
'the done can be undone but the undone can't be done'. Roaring
around the Burroughs but never in cabs and always smashed,
some combination of buzz and drowse in constant play
in my bloodstream, lights blurring past like perpetual North

Stars. My days dazed in amazement. The idea of true north held no interest. I was knocking back scotches with a guy who knew a girl whose roommate I had dated, was playing pool with George Plimpton and clubbing to jungle, was being invited out to Fire Island and could call a smash single before anyone but the record execs. How I roared!

Now I take Metro North into the city and do my roaring around in a hybrid car with a car seat but that's north of nevermind. Say I'm using a knife's blunt edge to smash garlic for a marinara sauce I'd wager better than the guy who says 'Bam! Kick it up a notch!' No matter who I was, I'm happy, have no other choice in the next act of the play.

I still like to see things smash. More or less, I am that guy. But all that bluster and roaring is like belief in Santa's North Pole into adolescence. Not what was and will stay in play.

On Why I Hate Bananas

Haibun for Krip Yuson

Suppose we all have certain foods or odors, like turnips or white wine vinegar, that turn our stomachs but in most gastronomical matters, I strive to be a pluralist. When it comes to bananas though, I can make no exception. Just the sight of them, blotched with sarcoma like on an old man's wattle or sliced into slimy half-moons that peek between flakes and milk, makes me avert my eyes. Obviously the Freudians among you will cite shape but it's more than that. I have a distinct memory of the moment of unconcealment when as a child I opened my lunchbox and took out an overripe banana to bite into its flesh, only to discover the true nature of disgust. When I was in the Philippines, I was told the banana plant in folklore had grown from the severed arm of a thwarted lover, buried in the ground until it sprouted yellow fingers. Second year of college, bored and broke, we took to bending reality on the cheap, gagging down cough syrup for the dextramorphine and once smoking the skin scraped from inside a banana peel, a noxious fume that still fills my lung with urge to convulse. My father, it should be noted, considers the banana, the 'perfect fruit', because he has thrift and cleanliness issues and is glad to eat something that no one else's hand has handled and that he can buy for less than a dollar a pound. The world's most grown crop in output by weight and as fate would have it, India leads the world's production, nearly doubling the output of Brazil, its next nearest competitor. There it's used in *halwas*, blended in *raitas*, fried into *vadas*, eaten raw as plantains and prescribed as panacea for heartburn, nerves, ulcers, PMS and mosquito bites. But it's not just an Asian thing, *nahi no*, the fruit has been the source of one of the great trade disputes between the US and Europe, a war waged in the 1990s over tariffs, free trade and the legacy of colonial history. Remember banana republics before they sold chinos? For every dollar spent on bananas at the supermarket, about a nickel goes to the plantations, which in turn is divided up even further before the migrant workers see a cent. Pumped full with pesticides and agrochemcials, grown on land specifically cleared by transnational fruit corporations, sucking the soil dry of nutrients by leaving no leaf litter, producing more waste and carbon dioxide emission than any other crop, once the banana tree has fruited, its crop picked over for aesthetic perfection, the plantation is abandoned to decompose into fiber and frond before it's onto the next deforestation. Every five years or so, having been piled on incessantly by the bananaphiles and beginning to doubt myself what seems such an odd and irrational aversion, I will again try a piece of banana bread or a banana split heaped with fudge and ice cream and each time, I will gag, wondering how I could have forgotten. Potassium and B12 be damned! Dear friends, whether Cavendish or Manzana, fresh or dried, overripe or still green, the jaundiced phallus, King Banana, has ruled our palate for much too long. Let's take a stand against these vile emanations. Leave them to rot in Lady Chiquita's headdress and in the mouths of monkeys. Pray they point their cowardly fingers earthwards and yellow back into an arm.

Spotted with NAFTA
rot-fleck, genus Musa will
not mush in my mouth!

Barter

for Catherine Barnett

Possessed of some rudimentary detection skills,
I can spot a Rothko or a liar at twenty paces.
Can panfry dosas, walk on rooftops, misplace bills

in the most obvious places, clutter open spaces
with dog-eared books or newspaper clippings.
I've been known to win at cards or in most races

like upon the blacktop during recess, zipping
to snatch a chalk eraser. Can speak, if soused,
in decent French & remain adept at equipping

friends for a camping trip. Have even roused
flame from flint & steel, still know my knots
from clove hitch to bowline & when housed

by a friend, I know enough that dinner's bought
by me. Could, if pressed, construct metafiction,
elaborate fun house mirrors of prose that cannot

be turned into a movie. Have worked construction,
broken floors with a jackhammer. Sold knives
one summer to suburban housewives, using diction

of tang & rivet. Can dispense a kiss that survives
the lips, solve algebraic equations & score goals
in soccer. Say I've taken the shape of many lives.

The Melancholy of Shadows at Dawn

Along the banks of the Pearl River
where ghostly outlines of buildings materialise
in the polluted smog, I could just disappear
with the old men doing T'ai Chi and selling turtles
in rusty buckets, hawking stringy phlegm
into the river. I can barely see myself reflected;
my lover, daughters, mother plunge
through me, wispy as shepherd's purse
blanched in boiling water before filling
the wonton dumplings that wrinkle
like my baby girls' hands once wrapped around
my fingers, grasping so tightly,
and I swore I would never ever let go.
They are all that hold me to this earth.

They are all that hold me to this earth
and I swore I would never ever let go,
my fingers grasping so tightly,
like my baby girls' hands once wrapped around
the wonton dumplings that wrinkle,
blanched in boiling water before filling.
Through me, wispy as shepherd's purse,
my lover, daughters, mother plunge
into the river; I can barely see myself reflected
in rusty buckets, hawking stringy phlegm
with the old men doing T'ai Chi and selling turtles
in the polluted smog. I could just disappear
where ghostly outlines of buildings materialise
along the banks of the Pearl River.

Voyages

The imaged Word, it is, that holds
Hushed willows anchored in its glow.
It is the unbetrayable reply
Whose accent no farewell can know.
—Hart Crane

Breast Feeding at the Blue Mosque

Hidden from a queue to bag shoes a woman nurses a child
under a wool scarf in the shadow two fluted minarets cast
pitched towards incessant sun, a necessity somehow an insult
to *sharia* law, no matter what sustenance a lemonwedge
of breast, God's own, yields, puckering a tiny mouth
until bright eyes glaze to doll loll. Fairly alien to ponder
raw biology of milk conveyed by ducts lined with capillaries,
made from pouring stuff of stars: nourishment that manifests
minerals for bone from pulsing light.
                        Too close to the slickheat pushing out
between the legs of nearly every woman not your wife
but her as well? How could it be that her very being derives
solely from her relation to you, that she could have no value
in the calculus but to function as temptation, or its dome-
blue corollary, disappointment? No cover covers up
those integers holding the place of zeroes, Iznik tiles or after-
life virgins. Ostrich eggs on chandeliers don't dissuade spiders.
If the fear of the Lord is not the beginning of our wisdom,
then *La ilah ha il Allah* is a breast in a mouth, else nothing is.

Resurrection Song

*...we found at this place the rancheria of the Indians of the Payaya
nation. This is a very large nation and the country where they live is
very fine. I called this place San Antonio de Padua, because it was his
day. In the language of the Indians it is called Yanaguana...*
—From the diary of Father Damian Massanet from June 13, 1691

Imagine St. Anthony of Padua, the patron saint of lost things,
had not died prematurely of ergotism under the branches

of a walnut tree in 13th century Italy, but rather had lived
to dance the fandango in the accordion-driven *conjunto*

music of working class Mexicans along the wide riverbanks
of the city named for his feast day, where today you can sit

dipping fried quail into savory pecan butter and sip salted
margaritas, watching the sun set over the *Paseo del Rio*.

Imagine his encounter with the original stewards of this land.
What would he have given and what received in return?

According to Catholic legend, St. Anthony was possessed
of the miracle of bilocation, of being in two places at once,

simultaneously preaching in one Church and singing canticles
in a monastery many miles away, so it's not hard to picture him

both in the Old World and the New, sharing in a meal of oblong
prickly pears, gathered by Payaya Indians, rubbed in the sand

to remove its spines, and mashed into a paste to fill the mouth
with gratitude, for what blooms greenly, even in arid desert land.

Here's a prayer for what those Payaya's lost in their exchange
with the Spaniards: their language, their land, their buffalo,

their religion. The price of their souls could not have been worth
the cost of the Holy Eucharist, and no Mission seems sufficient

to salvage what was occupied, then discarded like flung seeds.
Thirty years after St. Anthony had and been buried, his vault

was apparently opened, revealing a body deteriorated to dust,
except for his tongue, which remained intact and incorruptible.

It's with that tongue, our tongue, the tongue of San Antonio
that we can sing the Native peoples—and ourselves—back to life.

South of Hebron

Across the onion fields, a hulk of rusted metal groans,
as out of place, it seems to the boy whose father tills
the land, as an orange blossom unfurling in a smokestack,
but there it is regardless, its turret swiveling like a broken
carousel, leaving a streak of flattened stalks in its wake.
The boy lives here. Picks his way probingly around traces
of mines to hear his language spoken in collapsible stalls
of the village market's measly remains. He has nothing
to hurl in his house, has to scour bulldozed quarries
for fist-sized rocks that slice heavily through the air,
meeting stray man or metal with satisfying thwack.
How small the rock is compared to the singular burden
of being made unwanted in a land you were born in,
for perpetuity, for no reason you will ever understand.

Before Sunrise, San Francisco

Bruno's by sallow candlelight,
the jacketed barkeep counting
tips from a jam jar and horseshoe
booths burnished a bit too bright,

yet the stained mahogany walls
and the lazy lament of spanish
horns from speakers huddled
in the corner speak a different

language altogether, one that rolls
effortlessly off the tongue and fills
the room like myrrh, a promise sent
that four walls can indeed keep out

the world, that when horns wail
for percussion and those walls
are elegantly attired, why there
is no need to ponder the gristle

in the mission outside, no need
to wonder why that one left you
or why you are always too
late. The weight of your existence

roughly equals the martini glass
in front of you, the thick mass
of the past collapses into brightness
as well-lit as the dripping star

at the center of your table.
Nod. Snap your fingers. Order
another drink. Let horns grieve,
let the wristwatch think on sheep

before you leave. Tonight,
the only eyes on you are two
pimentos stuffed into olives
bloated with vermouth and gin.

Small Town Catechism

for David Cappella

His cedar barn reeks of anise and gasoline,
a riot of tires loosely circumscribing its perimeter,
any vision of metropolis two thruways and a train
away or nodding through static on the tube.
However he hopes to pare himself, it's enough

to remain a fixture, like a garden implement
in the grass, turning surely into a truer self of rust.
His wife pots herbs into soil, but won't suck
him off the way he likes, even when a stone
wall lies between them and the nearest neighbor.

When he tells the story of his life to himself,
it's not cinematic, but withheld in abeyance
to some curve of space that claims his home
an unforgotten fleck in distant spokes of stars.
If things are how he says they are, who knows?

The Spirit Level

Hard hittin' New Britain, some of my students intone
to describe their home for a few years or a lifetime
in that depressed part of Hartford County once known

by relics in unphotographable pre-European times
as a fertile hunting and fishing ground by the Tunxis,
Quinnipiac, Wangunk, Podunk and Mattabesett tribes

who chipped arrowheads from coarse-grained schist,
naming the land Pagonischaumishaug, or White Oak Place,
though to say this in class, *please professor don't flunk us*

if we can't pronounce that, is what with a straight face
I get in response to evoking memories of these stewards
who seemingly have vanished without the faintest trace.

When English puritans left the King in droves towards
a place they could freely practice their religion without
persecution, they claimed that what they had explored

was *discovery,* and their own, no need to hammer out
a treaty by the ember of tallow candle or oil lamp,
it was theirs by divine fiat, till flash flood or drought

might eradicate them. So they settled a permanent camp.
Others followed, hemmed in by the Lamentation Mtns.
calling the region outside Hartford the 'Great Swamp'.

Two Scottish brothers set up shop, men with countenances
like the Amish we are lead to believe, tinners by trade
who'd import metal from Boston to make plates, buttons,

and spindles to sell on the road, transported and displayed
in a hand-cart. The original Yankee Peddlers, now a pawn
shop on Main Street where you can buy a used suede

jacket and a four-string, then eat lo mein at a faux-Sichuan
take-out down the road. By 1806, Eli Terry had the first
clock factory in America cranking out a large spawn

of interchangeable parts made of brass, and he dispersed
hawkers to sell the wares, thus evolving manufacturing.
Their recent farmer ancestors may well have cursed

their dumb luck to have been born toiling and fracturing
the soil by plow, when their grandchildren's grandchildren
shaped wire, wrought iron into shutter hinges, picturing

themselves as citizens of 'Hardware City', no longer sylvan,
but proudly urban, even starting to produce ball bearings.
Yes damn lucky, even if they didn't yet have cars or penicillin,

for those were on their way & Stanley Toolworks was hiring,
especially if you were a recent Polish Catholic immigrant.
Now many of the factories, if even still running, are firing

their remaining workers without the union's consent,
boarding up fire-prone buildings, padlocking the gates,
as some single mother of four can't afford to pay her rent

and in alleyway grime there are men asleep on grates.
What turned New Britski into an annex of the rust belt?
Why such dearth in one of the country's richest states?

According to the recent census, the downturn's felt
more by the select many, a cop's average yearly wage
north of seventy grand while those who once smelt

iron ore to make hand-crafted tools are now at an age
where their craftsmanship seems the stuff of dream,
where a thriving industrial past has been exchanged

for an average per capita income that must surely seem
even less than it actually is. No jobs. No more Tool Town.
Still the locals gather to watch the local baseball team,

the Rock Cats, and a resolute toughness still abounds.
Puerto Ricans have moved in, and the smell of *morcilla*—
sausage stuffed with pig's blood, rice, and spices, brown

as the families who eat it—wafts in the summer, Miller
High Life open on the stoop of the bodega as the kids
skip double dutch. The motto of faster, better, bigger

seems to have realised its own limitations. Now in fits
and starts, taking a cue from *Les Chasseurs Alpins*,
the French soldiers from World War I (not the Swiss

as some like to claim), intrepid mountaineers with hands
hid in capes, immortalised by Irving Berlin as Blue Devils,
not Duke's but Central's, a new demographic demands

better treatment. Take the well-made sliding T bevel
you might use to round a corner, or the plane, handsaw,
chisel, hammer, mitre box or aptly named spirit level

that uses an air bubble trapped in alcohol to reveal a flaw
in measurement, whether something is crooked or just
right, plumb fit for support. Where's a like tool for our law

books, to help frame zoning and tax codes? Scour the rust
from our eyes Saint Adalbert, allow us to cooperate with Pole
and Puerto Rican alike, remind us that fabricated from dust,

to dust motes we shall return, and teach us to love coal
black as much as we love white milk. It's long past time.
There was always someone in charge of quality control

at the factories, a supervisor whose job it was to supply
well-made goods to the consumer. Let's each become
our own best product. Let's love one another until we die.

Return to Mumbai

Bombay no longer, the island
circumscribed by water exhausts
herself in rain. for six months,

her suitors, vasai, ulhas, thane,
spar, each swelling, vigorously
surging, empurpling against

the horizon's taut washboard.
She, placid, stares breathless,
smiles the smile of a schoolgirl

whose step-father has just left
for london and decidedly opens
to each. Already, her soil soaks.

Already she sings in preparation,
rust-colored flames smoldering
compost, plastic tarps flapping,

held down by planks, stones,
discarded tires; dirt roads gravid
with rickshaws, vegetable wallahs

whipping bullocks, tata trucks
distended with diesel, yellow
and black taxis like so many drones

evacuating the hive, bicycles,
Ambassadors, Maruti Suzikis,
creaking double decker buses

emblazoned with the latest
Bollywood star, women in fraying
saris, barefoot men collecting

alms, children praying, their shape
more rail than real. From an island
mother, rising water fathers

this mitotic *bharathanatyam*,
an embryonic dance held
until the obstetrician's arrival.

Before Monsoon

Heat so oppressive that stray dogs
only lift their heads towards the butcher
shop where a cleaver thumps,
before settling back down under a goods

carrier or the shade of a thatched shack
which announces in large, arsenic
green block letters, 'Lifetime cures
for piles or fistulas'.

A rickshaw driver has wrapped his face
with a soaking *dhoti* and lies supine
in the back seat, refusing to take fares
while flies swarm thickly around a mound

of garbage a bearded ragpicker sorts
through with a blunt sapling,
preserving the odd item, preferably edible,
in a fibrous sack slung upon his back.

The golden rule here is inefficiency:
streets littered with half-begun houses
long-abandoned to a patina of red dust,
queues snaking in front of both clinic

and cinema, never seeming to advance,
men without protective headgear
hammering at a massive concrete flyover
while potholes gape in the crumbling road

a family of Jains bundled in white robes
crosses, their mouths covered to keep
out insects, their possessions balanced
upon their heads. How the sublime spills

into the scatological here with no apparent
contradiction, shrines popping up
from the grime of overpopulation
like toadstools after rainfall, a Ganesha

delicately carved in terracotta bobbing
on the dashboard of a truck that hauls
cow dung to villagers who use it for fuel,
a garland *wallah* doing brisk business

selling lotus flowers in an alleyway damp
with fresh urine. How the city points out
evidence of a seamless continuum:
heavens, earth, underworld—conjoint.

Sunrise over Angkor Wat

pathya vat for Minh Bui Jones

The pathya vat
is four beats long
a Khmer song
that bangs the thon

crow calls and grief
will not succumb
a tro *to strum*
our distant names—

We move through half-dark in the *tuk tuk*
our guide remarks to better call a remorque,
that French word for a trailer, the torque
of which pulls us close in sticky pre-dawn

that thickens with tourists of every flag,
rubbing sleep from their eyes to switch on
screens, unrolling blankets to sit upon,
lining the reflecting pool over which the sun

will soon appear. That's why we're all here.
To grow as close to being a monk or a nun
as we'll come, rooted in boots to stunned
silence, colour doing violence to obscurity

one creeping orange nanosecond at a time.
Consider the vast perpetual insecurity
of life on the Tonlé Sap, its exotic purity,
the Khmer people living in floating huts

when the lake floods during rainy season.
Unseen, unmemorialised, raw with cuts
from handling stone where cashew nuts
grew in groves, where are the many hands

of the labourers who so grandly incarnated
King Suryavarman II's vision of holy lands?
Only Vishnu, carved from sandstone, stands
under a saffron parasol made from sheerest

silk, to preside over Mount Meru on Earth.
From his most distant body to who's nearest,
suddenly we are all suffused with the clearest
morning imaginable. Time the temple shines.

The Cyprus Problem

canzone for Francesca Cauchi

Not the infamous 'green line' that bisects this miniscule island
on the Med—3/5th the size of Connecticut—and thought to be settled
in the Stone Age by hypothesised tribes who eschewed highland
to hunker down with pygmy hippos long extinct from the island
& build round houses with floors of terrazzo & burned lime.
Not the Turks & Greeks each claiming possession of the island
with two flags, two currencies, two languages, but just one island.
Not the UN peace-keepers called beach-keepers by the natives,
roaring around in white pick-ups when not trying to pick up the natives.
Not the fact that Roman politician Mark Antony once gave the island
as a gift to Cleopatra, nor that the apostle Paul wandered to convert
the population to Christianity. Not the Cypriot Muslim converts.

Not Ptolemy. Not Richard the Lionheart. Not the Cyprus pound converted
into the Euro. No the Cyprus problem is purely selfish: when I landed
at Ercan on land recognised by no one but Turkey, I couldn't convert
my dollars into Lira because the change place had been converted
into a kebab stall; couldn't find my driver because he had settled
into a cigarette & a Turkish coffee; couldn't find anyone to exert
the effort to speak English. Fatigued, confused, too slow to convert
to the Mediterranean pace of life where an hour late is being on time,
when I finally arrived at the flat, the refrigerator was specked like a lime
turned to rot, kaleidoscopic with spores, the floor & sill converted
into a disco for dust motes. Later colleagues assured me that the native
state is disarray & that things transpired in the most vegetative

way, if they transpired at all. Why I haplessly believed the native
mode of life was luxuriating on the beach & drinking frosty island
rum drinks, I have no clue. Must have to do with being a non-native
who projected illusions onto the land. But soon I became native

enough, a true denizen of *Kıbrıs*, the Turkish word for this island,
ordering *mezes* of grilled halloumi cheese, *dolmas* wrapped by native
fingers & drinking as much Efes & *ayran* as any other native.
I smoked lemon-mint tobacco from the hose of a *nargila* & settled
the bill by declaring '*hesap lütfen*'. Eventually I even found myself settled
into the flat, putting up *nazars*, pendants of evil eyes like other natives,
buying water by the five gallon, using bitter lemons in recipes where lime
was called for, opening the windows at dusk so that light could climb

up the trellis until the sky yawed like a freshly unearthed quarry of lime-
stone: sandy, gray & red-veined. But it was all a lie. There are no natives.
There are the Turks, Turkish Cypriots for whom call to *muezzin* is high time
for cocktails & London Cypriots found bemoaning the lack of limes,
mushy peas & fried fish. There are the Greek Cypriots, maybe converts
to the Anglican, else part of the Orthodox Church whose apparent line
of origin extends back to Jesus via unbroken Apostolic Succession. In time
one notices others: Armenians, Maronites, Iranians, émigrés to the island,
alongside Brits & descendants of the Lusignans or Venetians. On the island
it's absurd to ask who came first or what belongs to whom. During what time?
While five armies patrol this sun-concussed land, nothing will be settled.
Far better to ignore politics and pretend that everything has been settled,

else live in fictions, with Othello's round unvarnished tale the setting
for which was Famagusta, else with honeygold spring air stilled in time
by Durrell, living under the Tree of Idleness in Bellapais before settling
in Sommières in the south of France where perhaps the most unsettled
question was whether the market on Place du Marché was out of native
strawberries vital to making a proper *coulis*. If nothing seems settled
by ignorance or fiction, there's the compounds where ex-pats have settled,
too loud lager louts whitish as mussels tugged from shells converting

their savings into concrete villas strung like wash on the line, convenient
in proximity to pub & to seaside; for some a perfect retirement setting.
How the map I smooth out on my desk won't name parts of the island:
The north shaded gray, marked 'Occupied Territory'. Splits the land.
How the city I've lived in has four names, none endemic to the island,
& painting a giant TRNC flag on the Five Finger Mountains settled
nothing. I think of how thickly groves of oranges grow here but never lime
& how all citrus was transplants brought by Arab merchants. Not native.
In no man's land sundering a star-shaped capitol city, I will never convert.

Post-pastoral

The clearest way into the Universe
is through a forest wilderness.
—John Muir

Crossings

Between forest & field, a threshold
like stepping from a cathedral into the street—
the quality of air alters, an eclipse lifts,

boundlessness opens, earth itself retextured
into weeds where woods once were.
Even planes of motion shift from vertical

navigation to horizontal quiescence:
there's a standing invitation to lie back
as sky's unpredictable theater proceeds.

Suspended in this ephemeral moment
after leaving a forest, before entering
a field, the nature of reality is revealed.

Oyster

Gnarled as cliff-face, two shells suctioned,
one snug in another to shape a rocky pear,
bluish, held together by a dark protein hinge,

content once in spatfall on a piling, changed
from free-swimming to inert life filtering
plankton from water, beating cilia. Dredged

firmaments of bread & brine now on ice
with lemon wedges in a fish stall window.
Soft, protandric pulsations in mantle skirts

made liquid to itself, turning males female
& back again, telling secrets that require
a knife to pry open & vinegar to serve.

Cascades

Eddies hasten in rivulets of foam that over
time will gnaw into ground rock sure as drill
bits, but now froth like a bridal veil tossed

from ferry to flail against algae-encrusted
outcroppings with the sound of a thousand
whispers modulating in urgency—*over again*

& onwards—how wind shears the surface
of planks of light to leave burbling rumors
that water in motion defies its own finitude.

There beyond a crook, increased *ad libitum*
into tumult, terror, sheer boundlessness—
a horsetail's giant, discordant spray roars.

Willard Pond

Across the pine-fringed pond, a loon croons
once, twice, easily three times it fills the air
with half-laugh, half-warning. Beautiful & alien

to share the planet with such emanations,
to recognise in a sound no classically trained
tenor could exactly produce, kinship, a sense

that the distance between the alternate
universes human & bird inhabit is smaller
than ever imagined & more astonishing.

The loon pierces misty dawn a final time.
Once the urge to possess the sound passes,
I plunge, headfirst, into shimmering water.

Yellow Blusher

Sodden with rainwater, the yellow-capped
mushroom has swollen, hangs over its thin stalk
so copiously, it appears the next drop of water

will prompt the entire venture to topple,
which is illusion, like the appearance of oneness
that's contradicted by a spongy underside,

network of papery layers, gills that hold up
the campanulate cap which comes off
as slime when rubbed by inquisitive fingertips.

This mottled, tenuous fungus, so easily snapped
from the soil, speaks in tongues the old growth
forest is not conversant in, except after rain.

Dark

Ten minutes ago, there was gray in the sky,
now there's none, not a splotch of contour
& when I walk, I listen for gravel to crunch

underfoot so I don't end tooth in bushes.
Darkness in New England has a flavour close
to anise, a texture plush as peat moss, fills

the ear with cricket chirps, creaks with trees
amending their branches, smells like inside
a new shoe when there's still tissue paper

crumpled in the toe, feeds full on paranoia,
bloats the walker with blind urge to run
summarily offset by the necessity to grope.

Blood

Marrow-sprung, eucharistic fount, black
pudding beaten in a bucket, kept
from coagulating, final taboo sopped

in a tampon or gargling from a slit
carotid artery, left to darken in air
like sunset stored in citrated vials

for transfusion, thimblefuls of grape
juice, wedding ring on a leach finger,
brackish foodstuff for the undead,

not wrung from turnips, no denser
than porter, it flows filtered forward,
pumps from valves until it clumps.

Buzzards

Gregarious in hunger, a flock of twenty
turn circles like whorls of barbed wire,
no spot below flown over uncanvassed.

The closer to death the closer they come,
waiting on wings with keen impatient
perseverance, dark blades lying in wake

until age or wound has turned canter
into carcass or near enough for them
to swoop scrupulous in benediction,

land hissing, hopping, tearing, gorging.
no portion, save bone, too durable
to digest. What matters cannot remain.

Peacock

Upon a corbelled stone wall, a thrall of eyes
peers from a train draped iridescent across
mid-afternoon, embroidered from Saturn's

rings perhaps, lustrous with crescent sheen,
burning bright blue & green like a dare
not to take seriously the premise of intelligent

design. How feathered audacity weighs
proportionally more than a bejewelled crown
upon a king's bald pate. What roving beak

knows it's festooned with a drum major's tom,
imperial & startling. When an ostentation
of birds constitutes an aesthetic unarguable.

Sounds

Depending on their shape, different rooms,
unoccupied, produce particular sounds
we lack a vocabulary for, gradations of silence

that turn ghostlier the higher the ceiling,
that deepen or disperse in echo the thicker
the surrounding foliage pressing against

whatever material the wall is made from,
whether fieldstone, brick, plaster, or wood.
To hear something without being able to name it

is a form of recovery & a source of frustration
which has at root an obsession with control
that can never be fulfilled, not in this lifetime.

Box Turtle

Jewelled egg in the middle of a twisting
path tamped down by footfall, darkened
in the shadow of tall pines, I pluck & put

it to my nose. Gradually, like arousal
rousing by degrees, a blunt head extends
from an uncircumcised prepuce to glare

red-eyed at how earth has been removed
from under it, how it flails three-toed
in space until, abruptly, a hinged plastron

snaps shut. Gathering itself in, domed shell
concentrically radiating orange & black
in a mantra: hermetic, tantric, self-reliant.

Bumblebee

How a well-machined hairy orb bobs yellow-
breeched philosophy: foraging optimally,
visiting the vertical inflorescences of foxglove

from bottom up, pumping palp & maxilla
with the precision of pistons, no wasted motion,
searching under the sepals of monkshood

like a furtive lover, or like a German engineer
in the heliotrope, loading full corbiculas
with sticky pollen, moving bloom to bloom,

then back to a comb lodged between springs
of a truck cab seat rusting in green rushes.
Back to dance an alphabet of honey & wax.

Slate

Slagheaps of stone once an ancient sea
floor, now metamorphosed into foliated
slabs that jut in cragged angles breakable

along two planes of cleavage & grain
by splitters who lounge with lunch pails
and idle pit hammers beside a rusted-out

compressor, eyeing us warily. In a haze
of dust, we trace the mottled texture,
gray-green flat enough to hone a knife on,

durable enough to use for sill & lintel,
billiard-table bed & grave marker. Nouns
unlike our fingers: resistant to weathering.

Ants

One is never alone. Saltwater taffy colored
beach blanket spread on a dirt outcropping
pocked with movement. Pell-mell tunneling,

black specks the specter of beard hairs swarm,
disappear, emerge, twitch, reverse course
to forage along my shin, painting pathways

with invisible pheromones that others take
up in ceaseless streams. Ordered disarray,
wingless expansionists form a colony mind,

no sense of self outside the nest, expending
summer to prepare for winter, droning on
through midday heat. I watch, repose, alone.

Mohegan Sun

Where Uncas once wore a wampum collar
hand-carved from purple quahog clamshells,
a mammoth anodised rose looms, reflective

& stainless off the interstate. *Come play!*
a bunting stretched over the road trumpets
and to descend the climate-controlled

elevators into the clockless gaming floor
pulsing with colour is to uncover a spectacle
broadcast on a wall of monitors: the fourth

circle of Hell, where avarice & excess
roll boulders back & forth, from Slotopoly
to the baccarat table. Time & again, I lose.

Dragonfly

Darting blue shard the length of a toothpick
with enough nerve & agility to mate in midair,
to snatch midges from a hovering swarm

faster than the purple martins will snatch it,
each blip in its fractal flight an insect eaten.
Compound eyes made from thousands of eyes,

motion in all direction, pale soft naiad bodies
hardened with exoskeleton, grown into wings
that shimmer afternoon with rapid translucence,

turning the planked boardwalk along the lake
into a darning needle's sketch of cross-stitches.
In time, they'll sew shut your eyelids & lips.

Double Rainbow

Speeding, without destination, after dark
torrents have poured & been returned
at home, the skies above mirror my mood,

windshield wipers knifing through sheets,
back roads slick with pooling, when a shard
of cloudlessness opens. Pulling over, cutting

the ignition, I unstitch myself from the humid
seat, still fuming, to greet a full spectrum
of colour arcing past the treetops in lockstep

with its fainter inverse. Archer's bow, hem
of the sun god's coat, bridge between worlds,
reconciliation & pardon. They don't last.

Fireflies

Heavy-draped beyond the slipform stone
wall laid one over two, two over one
& shimmed by thin fingers of granite,

night falls moonless in a bindweed field
stretching to a dark grove that flares light—
sudden, incessant, nitric—electric sea-green

bursts more frequently seen on an arcade
screen, signals a synchronous Morse code
of mating sent from lanterns rung in a rosette,

innervated by neurons, souls of the dead
in Japanese folkore, hotaru. Actually, it's love:
They only find each other in the dark.

Carnal Nature

The way you make love is the way God will be with
you.
—Rumi

Lucia

My hair, voluminous from sleeping in
six different positions, redolent with your scent,
helps me recall that last night was indeed real,

that it's possible for a bedspread to spawn
a watershed in the membrane that keeps us
shut in our own skins, mute without pleasure,

that I didn't just dream you into being.
You fit like a fig in the thick of my tongue,
give my hands their one true purpose,

find in my shoulder a groove for your head.
In a clinch, you're clenched and I'm pinched,
we're spooned, forked, wrenched, lynched

in a chestnut by a mob of our own making,
only to be resurrected to stage several revivals
that arise from slightest touch to thwart

deep sleep with necessities I never knew
I knew until meeting you a few days
or many distant, voluptuous lifetimes ago.

Paleontology's End

Sifting through teeth and carapaces
with a magnifying glass, you adopt
a hyperopic perspective, history
fermenting from what continually
ends to replenish itself. A peregrine
falcon's scapular is slowly eaten
by soil from which poke the spoke-
heads of late summer's dandelions
ten thousand years later. Permian,
Ordovician, Cretaceous, Devonian,
Triassic: we've named the major
eras of mass extinction. The past,
happening, has preserved its portion
in amber, in crenellated clamshells
and tree bark, to augur what we'll be
for posterity. Drop the horsehair
brush, permit the slides to drowse
in disinfectant, leave the bones;
someone warm lies waiting.

Ode to Quickies

Lunch hour. The time it takes
to meet in anonymity leaves
no more than forty minutes.
All preamble be damned:
hike up, hunker down, flush
the color of bruised peaches,
fall against casements in knots
of garment, tilt towards me,
so I'm exposed while you rove
a grove that grows in plums
with each sucked-in breath,
while wordless communiqués
flash between us, rapt to be
here, so roused beyond
the mere scope of skin,
only skin can suffice to hold
the charge of the rash
dance that fits the wan light
upon these chalky walls—
perfectly.

String Solo

Is it a sound, thrush-gasp or throaty whimper, you keep wrapped in wax paper for midwinter nights, two hands and a vowel for company? Do longed for fragments sing long enough to tilt wheel on axis, spill? Slipped strap, tippled glade, lace in fretwork, slow bloom of shoulder blade, clasps to unclasp, lamplight on hairsheen, orchids blooming at the wrists, gullies to swim in, the hour elongated, shivery, a smell to carry off on the thumb, peaty and overripe, but disappeared too soon, turned muzzy. Jutting into the hour like craving for marmalade, how thickened past touch the pastiche? An urgent, inclement burst of syrupy weather that drenches the doer in doing, a mellifluous, jagged syntax that when recalled will not be real, not even close? Will any ecstatic dust remain like cardamom between the fingers? *Camerado*, all I know is the cello in imagination makes music less sweet than hearing its body vibrate before us, clenched between knees, flayed by a bow, cradled at the base of the neck.

Surface Tension

Scarified now but how? When we once heard
parades from windows, swayed in artificially

luminescent reeds under the Brooklyn Bridge,
filled soaked corn husks with masa dough,

glimpsed mouse-deer scamper on wish-thin
legs, called each other *mon petit coeur de sucre*,

split each other like oranges at the navel,
turning pith to string between wet fingers.

Our realm was the back of doors, ill-lit alleys,
laying splayed out on a lake dock baked in sun

until the impulse to jump. We were gods
caught in a rising soap bubble, arms bare,

upswept scent of sand dune barren as moon
except for us twinned, intertwined, tied

to nothing but in the moment each other.
Where did you go? Suds, not love, evaporates.

Thought at Night

Nearly impossible to separate
the roof from the blacking weight
that presses in the screened-off windows
girding the perimeter of this dusty cupola—
every line here blurs as I chew

the insides of my chapped lips
to keep from inviting oblivion to hammer
blood into the moment's monumental
supremacy. The air between us dampens
under the spokes of my unshaved face,

lolls with the musk between your knees,
how easy it would be...
surrounded on all sides by obscurity
and not grace—you build nests
while words fly from my mouth like terns

plunging for prey iridescent beneath
the surf—since talking to you I am thinking
of betraying her, a thousand miles removed
from our conversation about truth
in lending, a banking term for laying

all your cards out face-up (the gaming
metaphor for the absence of games),
though the way you say it,
it seems to mean how we extend
credit to each other, loaning our bodies

on security, hoping to accrue
the greatest possible interest right now
not so much as later. the way you say it,
I understand all relationships
are about exchange. standing with my arms

crossed behind my back, I stare
at the great nothing of the roof and the trees,
slowly taking shape in the greater nothing
of night, wondering what to do with the dark
realisation that I don't belong to myself.

Lake with Human Love

for Michel Weisberg & Sharon Pacuk

Seen from canoe stem on a moonless night
the cosmos stretches boundlessly above,
a panoply of stars & the whitish curve
of the Milky Way, leaving the lone paddler

significantly insignificant, utterly diminutive
yet part of some larger, grander tapestry
unable to fully fathom. Human love is like
that, for when it appears, it affirms the person

before us, not as a projection or a romantic
ideal, but as who our beloved in actuality *is*.
When you love, it is paradoxically not you
who love but love which acts through you,

imbuing the mortal life with divine purpose.
The stars & the lake are one with the craft
moving through the water & the letter *J*
being inscribed in an eddy only to dissolve

& be written over again & again is one
with the breath of a body stilled into motion,
& the midnight excursion & landscape
it takes place in are metaphors for the union

of two souls who are companions & lovers
& friends. There's the real physical work
it takes to move forward, the synchronicity
in the curve of moon, intermittent headwind

rippling shadows & startling loon-cries,
all flowing both outwards & inwards
at once, not manmade nor projected from
the ego, but really there & revealed to us

in small daily acts of relatedness that help
texture the mysterious fabric of our lives.
Then there's the solitary figure in the canoe,
alone because one must be self-sufficient

before becoming successfully part of a pair,
yet not alone because everything conspires
to claim otherwise. Say somewhere around
the bend the beloved waits, not to be loved

but to love, not to fulfill desire but to move
beyond it, not to possess but to share with
like the living pact between space & time,
water & craft, that brings us together as one.

How Excursions Can Rupture Time

for Michelle Cahill

Reading Cavafy here, a lakeside thick with mist,
I return not for the first time to the sultry heat
that lit up the rickshaw and the sense of escape

we shared in Mumbai, away from the academics
and poets, uncoiled from contraption for a fierce
instant, as if these moments stitched alongside

our quotidian lives are realer, more intensified
and rare as certain birds that live in deep jungle.
The central conceit in 'Longing' is a sumptuous

mausoleum where beautiful, too-young corpses
molder, like unfulfilled desire not given its night
or radiant morning, which I find both quite apt

and intrinsically flawed when I think of hurtling
together, infinitely possible in a yellow meteor,
speaking about ourselves intimately, uninhibitedly,

walking through the crowded streets, anonymous,
into alleyways heaped with multicolored fabrics
and buzzing with flies, past that sign in English

for a book printer in front of which we snapped
your photograph, posing with writerly delight.
Apt because despite my best efforts, you drifted

in tanktop and backpack alone into the night,
nullifying some coefficient in the cosmic proof.
But flawed because such desire never ever dies.

That's its great appeal, why the Buddha saw it
at the root of all suffering, how want won't stop
wanting, but why I see it quickening the heart

of much art, veering towards truth and beauty
headlong like in a three-wheeler blindly headed
nowhere but towards this wild place between us.

Carousel

Singeing the heels of a quarrel,
another renewal, with what for fuel?

Is it courage or fear that brings us
both tears, each unable to leave the other?

Outside, the world displays its devices,
lures and entices, promises pleasures

earnest as arsenic and easier than rain.
Which must be why we refrain ... It's true,

that with you I'm shriven, but remember
when we were children, and joy

joy was a given.

Home Together

Between us the vacuum of early evening,
a pot of rice and beans simmering on the stove.
between us, for now, an easy domesticity,
the way we move past each other without words,
a thin breeze hitched up to bay windows,
our footsteps rattling on the hardwood floors.
words are there though, invisible yet sharp
as incisors pulled from a hound's drooling jaw,
words we can never have meant to speak,
but did, recanted, then spoke again.
such words should have died in our lungs.
they have staked between us a fence of teeth.

Misty Blue

Reared for the afternoon, the boutiques display
furniture, fur-coated mannequins, defunct signs
from a passed time, as we stroll along Broadway,
serene, until there's a mild censure, the saturnine
response, a harsher rebuke, my defensive thrust,
and soon we two, nearly grown one, are at war,
charged with anger that doesn't turn to lust
as it does in the movies. We stop at a parked car,
oblivious to the passing faces, and try to rip free
from the gravity that holds us, verifying love
as an algorithm of hate, something guaranteed
to hurt. Drained, we turn. Then as if from above
comes *Misty Blue,* a version Ella Fitzgerald sings.
The music, while it lasts, changes everything.

The Song to Kāmadeva, God of Love

In January hoarfrost, I sweep the ground
to draw sacred mandalas with fine sand,

intricate adornment of stars and matrixes
of dots in rice powder that will disperse

in the afternoon void. The art of engaging
beauty for its own form and transient sake.

Enraptured, flushed pink, I turn to you
& your brother to ask, how do we still live?

Tie me with the hand that holds the discus
ringed in fire so I might adorn more streets

with sand dripped through my fingertips.
I bathed alone during the vast song of dawn,

& tended the fire with tender, smooth twigs.
My vow to him courses through my body

like a ripened blossom strung on your bow
to release with keening motion the name

of the only one capable of ocean-breaths,
the Demon Slayer who dots us with song.

Draw the bow at me, loosening braids of reason
until I am an untied string without a knot,

united as wave and postulate. Concluded.
Three times a day I will worship at your feet

with fragrant blossoms of moonflowers,
my heart ablaze, from fiery tips of arrows

woven from efflorescence to spell his name,
Govinda, a musk essence of transcendence.

Aim the arrow at him & let it fly, to pierce
him until I might enter that succulent light.

O ancient Kāmadeva, I paint cave walls
with your names, trace with glistening

forefinger your banner bearing glinting fish,
attendants waving fly-whisks, your sleek

sugar cane bow shining with filigreed carvings.
Do you even take notice of my obsession?

From childhood, I pledged all that in time
would ripen and swell to the one and only

lord of Dwaraka; I beg you unite me with him.
My surging breasts long to leap to the touch

of his hand which holds aloft the flaming discus
& the conch. I shudder to think of my body

being offered to mortal men when it was made
to wait only for him, like prasad, the sacred

offering anointed by learned Brahmins versed
in the Vedas, but instead of being mingled

with the divine, to be sniffed & pawed at, desecrated
by forest jackals who'd eat decomposing bones

easily as blessings. Even through springtime,
I will keep my word Kāmadeva & praise you

for rousing the insatiable, sleep-heavy limbs
of maidens into exquisite mutual enticement.

All day, I will sit within myself, waiting for the dark
lord hued & arrayed overhead as rain clouds,

then as dusky blossoms from a blackberry bush.
Please coax his glance this way! Persuade his lotus-

eyes to consider my lithe bud, to shower down grace.
O Manmatha! Take my simple gifts: sugar-

cane, freshly harvested grains, steamed sweet rice,
flattened paddy; ask him to eat them from my hand.

Coax the world-measurer to caress my waist,
to encircle the twin globes of my breasts

& your glory will resound for generations to come.
See my body is filthy. My hair unravels. My lips pale.

I eat but once a day, grudgingly, already engorged
on longing. O radiant and mighty Kāmadeva.

The Many Uses of Mint

Fresh mint leaves muddled with cane sugar
at the bottom of a rocks glass full of crushed

ice and an exquisite spiced rum don't taste
as good as you, not even close, though sprigs,

intoxicant green and flavourful, spring to mind
when I think of you, consider your nape, flute-

shaped, and your almond eyes that see so far
into me that what I'm yet capable of surfaces

like wet earth gravid with the start of shoots
after a protracted frost has finally thawed.

Or say, I'm new minted in your gaze, unused,
unmarred, coined especially to fit your purse,

to be pawed, turned over, spent as legal tender
in a country whose borders no map could draw

because it extends past this life into the next,
into the past, where we were more verdant

than jade polished to a sheen, were the envy
of every hoarder's greed but could only belong

to each other because in each other we reach
the apotheosis of—dare I say it?—human love.

Then down to Scottish use it comes, *to attempt,*
to intend, to suggest, to dare, to make a mint

at it, no matter the impediments which run
beyond winter, past numismatists, clear of mites

that might gnaw a stem to a well-withered nub,
into infamy of the Capulet variety—*what indeed*

is in a name?—into a gale of forces that coalesce
to enforce such abstractions as 'sanctity'

and 'family values' even while the rafters quake.
Petrifying yes but fuck it—let's make a mint at it.

Phrase and Contour

If you have to ask what jazz is, you'll never know.
—Louis Armstrong

Broca's Area

with Nancy Kuhl

no beveled jewel jagged
rockface cliff edge where
mountain dreams itself
to mist from riverbed
no ancient fault line no
memory of catastrophe
only breath one enters
another departs this is
the perpetual discordance
between thinking and
thought an impossible
figure preserved groove
and catch fixed into flux
fossilised finalised a form
we almost recognise a feather
or bone the skin the shell
the body that intimate shape
like a name or any word
held too long on the tongue

The Living Trust Mill

with Jim Daniels

The discordance between thinking and thought
occurred just after the knockout punch
but before he hit the canvas.
Floodlights met deer in headlights,
mouthpiece a momentary parabola dripping spit
in camera flash and crowd roar. He had no shot
in any court of law. He was guilty, guilty,
and who couldn't count from one to ten?

Even the orphan child and the cute dog shook
their heads and walked away. Ambled out like amber waves
of green. Every payout had its outfit, even fitness
drinks debated in the boardroom were engorged on power-
point pie charts and a dream of MORE destination vacations
than any mere mortal could muster. Money in drinkable form,
dehydrated coins, capsulated dollar bills. Power, fitness,
fitness, power. *Gimme another piece of that pie. The one,*
the chewy one, the crunchy one, the juicy one.
The cartoon pie, the moon pie. The shy pie.
Gimme the last piece of the last pie. Not rarified words

like transnational and monetary policy. Just 'I'm going to get me mine',
like Keith Sweat crooned. Unfortunately
the moment is not just self-reflective, contains Gambians
unlit, unctuous with sweat, unregistered by green card,
scouring pots in the basement of a French Bistro
in the meatpacking district. Like Keith Croon sweating
and swearing, scouring and glowering, some giant Somebody
pinching out their light like a nubby candle
after a long night of quiet wine, the solemn ceremony

of obliteration, limbs and teeth lulled to sleep.
The holy relic of the green card, a sliver of the one true green card
wrapped in tissue, lifted to a place of solitary worship, the absurdly clean
hands praying for a worthy scam. Like the man in a slick suit selling
annuities to men in plaid pants: Fixed, immediate, variable, deferred,
equity-indexed. New forms for bilking. We're all grist for the living trust
mill. How much would you pay

someone not to be paid to clean ditches and bale crops
in Death Valley midday? Just sign on the dotted line,
an X is fine. Stick, stack, sloe-eyed seamstress
in a sweatshop while bee-bop skittles on no radio station in earshot. Just
the drone of needles. Hope evaporating into gray sky's hollow drone. A
man rocking on a stoop closes his eyes and remembers vision.

Imagine someone whittling his bones for kindling
or to carve an even smaller man. Imagine someone
calling this a job. Instead, while wayang puppets dance punch-drunk,
imagine the seven tones of metallophones, bamboo flutes and brass gongs
that comprise the gamelan. From the Javanese 'to hammer'. Shimmered
sound
the frequency of a distant planet's orbit.
A communal act, job of another hue.

The sun bites into our small rotations of hope.
We shade our eyes against it. We steer our spaceships
toward dazzling music, the sweet darkness where all
is lost. Keening oboe and bassoon obbligati.
Boosters and fuel tanks dropping through atmosphere
to ocean floor, shard of ship receding into pulsating

reaches of nothingness. How the fact of its trajectory
shares an event horizon with both chauffeured
man and dark man who cleans out the discharge
cylinders of slurry pumps, then leaves in a rented van.
The chauffeured man is deep in thought.
The dark man is thinking.

Savagery

with Eileen Myles

The castle looms blue
upon the porcelain plate
soon it began quacking,
quivering like perpetually—
in-motion Jell-O, all hue
and rainbow jiggle.
All spinning like tops.
Inside was another story
However. Moths fought.
Protein-packed
flagrant little paper
weights using head
lights for celestial
navigation

The Shanty of Subliminal Governance

with Megan Levad

give me wings
and a wagon wheel for a buckle
and a rattlesnake for a toothpick
and a fastidious mule
my amanuensis
before we set out to explore this new country
of which I have always already been
the final and most fair
emperor
give me wings
and a winking god
with a set of dice
that has more sides than an electron
in a masked ball
of inertial space
a gyroscope that wobbles in place:

take my dictation in loopy script
and longitude in decimal degrees
and dare me to wonder
my peripatetic monk
my monkey, my money, my honey
lazed into mint tea, find x
in relation to me, to the
You Are Here
spot dragged along
beneath us as long
as we have bodies to take
up space: place
a penny on my eyes

to surmise sleep
proffer copper for boat fare
for Charon's obol orbiting
the sacrament of mind looking
back at the slack flesh
with a wish to be two
but not two:

Why Do I Have to Have a Body?
and: If I Do, Why Can't I Lie
Back and Enjoy It, this muse, medium
for touch and taste, wily wedding
of muscle and bit to master
and serve pale horse and rider
myth and the tongue to speak it
in eloquent if garbled syntax
a glossolalia of grunt and gesture
believed by Cessationists to be a cloud
of unknowing that shudders
in a frontal lobe lightning storm
of song no errant tremulous jay
can decipher though its fire
still burns the fingertip which longs
to linger longer to feel something
fiercer than flame, a nourishment:

if you feed us
we'll forget how to feed ourselves
but that's the big idea,
making forgetting a function

like the face of the surgeon
upon incision or the cook
lost in a haze of reduction
if we forget you,
we will imagine we planted
the big idea ourselves.

The New Rodeo Lexicon

mistranslated glossary for Tim Sandlin

Added Money
Budget Deficit = Net Savings + Trade Deficit − Investment

Aggregate
net result of knowing and applying all defined terms. Not to be confused with composite materials or news tickers.

Arm Jerker
to marketing and promotion what *Les Parapluies de Cherbourg* is to handkerchiefs.

Association Saddle

1.1 The principal Sitter shall be as set forth in the Articles of Organisation. These By-Laws, the powers in all matters concerning conduct and regulation, the duration and quality of the Sitting and any damage that might therewith ensue shall be subject to such provisions in regard thereto, if any, as are set forth in the Articles of Organisation as from time to time in effect.

2.1 The members of the Association in Competition are its Adhering Bodies.

2.2 Only under extraordinary circumstances might the Association admit a suitably designated additional Adhering Body to take the place of the original Sitter. A Sitter may appoint as proxy only an adult member of his or her household weighing as much as but no more than the Sitter at weigh-in.

2.3 The Rump in question will be owned and controlled by the Sitter, who takes full responsibility for the salubrious or injurious effects that result from the Sitting.

3.1 Any rights of copyright hereunder shall not be exclusive and can be virally transmitted in video, photo and textual form to any number of print or electronic media outlets or private owned lists that the Association may ordain suitable, thereby marketing the product to the fullest. Any nonmonetary gains shall accrue directly to the memories of the Adhering Bodies.

Ball Out
sudden burst of chutzpah, bravura or sisu in the waning moments of any endeavor

Bareback Riding
raw man on man action for pigs, bears, cubs and twinks.

Bareback Rigging
staging the aforementioned on camera.

Barrier
1. a fence of sensors and spotlights along the Mexican border.
2. an exploit once known as mooning.

Barrel Racing
dissembling the staves back into oak and the hoops back into ore.

Body Roll
sagging so low you could see our boxers, yo!

Boot the Bull
giving up the thorny path of prevarication to let the light of Jesus shine into your life.

Break Away Calf Roping
application of a synergistic blend of lanolin, beeswax and colloidal silver in ointment form to relieve the pain, itching and inflammation.

Break Away Roping
Tarzan-like escape from a rehab clinic with vines or cables.

Buford or Pup
born blind and deaf in a litter among the thugs.

Bull Riding
variable speed buck and spin control in custom hides. Also known as
taming 'the bucking machine". See: John Travolta and Debra Winger.

Calf Roping (on Foot)
thickened areas of dead skin painful to put pressure on.

Cantle Boarding
a synergy of paraffin fakie frontsides and aromatherapy nose grabs,
harnessing the wick to the extreme!

Catch as Catch Can
some combination of grappling, hair tearing, fish-hooking, groin clawing,
sternum elbowing, eye gouging, lip tearing, kidney thumping, ear
biting, nerve numbing, stomping and pummeling that prepares one for
reconstructive surgery or the mixed martial arts.

Chute Dogging
one of the basic tenets of Freeganism, or 'limited participation in the
conventional economy and minimal consumption of resources". Also
known as binning, alley surfing, curbing, shopping at the D-mart, garbage
gleaning, dump-weaseling, tatting, skally-wagging or trashing.

Community Loop
Yves confessed to Man who chided Max who was fucking Joan who
hadn't told André he wasn't straight but had implied as much to René
while berating Luis for not inviting Marcel as they all drove to Yves'
house for a dinner party.

Cover
a fake moustache or heavy metal ballad performed with harmonica and
Moog synthesisers.

Cross Fire
early film noir.

Cutting
four times as many females than males have used sharp edged objects in
self-harm then worn turtlenecks and long sleeves to hide the evidence.

Cutting Pen
the bathroom mirror.

Dallying Off (Dally)
spending a workday lunch in the park for too long dreaming of being an
urbane bon vivant having an affair with a minimum wage honey to take
the mind off its troubles.

Daylighting
far in the daylight haze among the piles
as of some fed up drone sacked out by lunch
when all is dull, and task and day with wail
pass too slowly to even put off doing work
          (after Tennyson's 'The Passing of Arthur')

Dogfall
a windfall gain that comes with a concomitant burden that makes its
value dubious. Like an unexpected inheritance that is not monetary but
in the form of a pit bull kennel, complete with leather leashes, syringes,
pry bars, breeding stand and explicit instructions prohibiting a sale.

Dogging
banging a stranger in public or talking smack behind someone's back.
Not to be confused with prairie dogging.

Dragger or Trotter
piece of refuse like masking tape or leaf with sap on it that clings to the shoe.

Fading
(from Phaedrus' treatment at the hands of Socrates) to dismiss or to mock. As in 'I faded the fool right to his momma's face'.

Fanning
going on a blitz shopping for clothes with your team's logo, buying season tickets, listening to sports talk radio, and meditating on such bits of gospel as 'when your running game is nor working, you've got to go to the air'.

Flag Racing
1. first one to the top of the pole gets the worst abrasions.
2. an oxymoron like a Cherokee Pioneer or freezer burn. See also: the flagging race and steer riding.

Fleaster
the most important feast in the Wingless Insect liturgical year, celebrated in observance of the fact that from the cycle of larva, pupa and imago, new larva is constantly produced. Secular celebrations involve the capering of a Fleaster Bunny.

Floating
perpetually leaving one or two major requirements undone so graduation day is put off for as long as possible.

Freight Trained
being interrupted while in the process of saying something particularly witty.

Goat Dressing
1 stick butter
2 cloves of fresh garlic, minced
1 teaspoon lime juice
1 tablespoon soy sauce
1 tablespoon Worcestershire sauce
1 tablespoon celery salt
1/2 teaspoon each, rosemary, basil, savory and oregano
1/2 teaspoon black pepper

Hat Bender
something so strange that it boggles the mind to contemplate. Like the
international curiosity in Britney Spears.

Hazer
one responsible for the procurement of goats, duct tape, paddles,
pantyhose and tasers.

Headhunter
nickname for a military recruiter.

Hickeyed
not as pumpkin pie-eyed as the bumpkin or bleared with whiskey as the
redneck but specked with the colourful pleasures of the hog farm.

Hot-Shot
        (disambiguation) a generic term that describe all types of electric
        shocking devices.
        (disambiguation) solid iron cannonballs heated, then fired from
        cannon
bacteria that's invaded the bladder. Can be tested for with a swab.

Hung Up
progression from attraction to idealisation, from anxiety to fear of
abandonment, from tunnel vision to stalking.

Lap and Tap
1. segueing from a Blaze Starr to a Fred Astaire number.
2. victory celebration of a championship swimmer that involves aquatic sex.
3. drinking water out of a dog bowl and begging for more.

Lounger
made of perspex acrylic complete with backrest that adjusts from full upright to horizontal and pull-out tray to hold cocktails. Uses industrial strength magnetism to offer a genuine floating sensation and no-fixed-means-of-support.

Marking Out (Marked Out)
use of the teeth in kissing to particularly noisy effect. Best done with clash of braces. Once one's teeth are sore, one is officially considered to be 'marked out'.

Mash Up
to have humorous forms to call on if performance of the animal is inferior, like the 'feast of fools' (*festa sultorum*) and free 'Easter laughter' (*risus pasachalis*). This is not a spectacle seen by the people; they live in it. Contestants who are 'no shows' for carnival festivities or who don't wear long-sleeve shirts, long pants, western hat, and boots that minimally cover the ankle and have a heel will be disqualified. Degradation, in the case of hindered performance in the stall, digs a bodily grave for a new birth. Whether fools or clowns. Goats or steers.
> (mash up of the International Gay Rodeo Association (IGRA) rules and Mikhail Bakhtin's *Rabelais and His World*. Translated by Helene Iswolsky)

Pegging
> (disambiguation) defining trait of Bob, or Bend-over boyfriend
> (disambiguation) to narrow cuff-size by folding over and rolling.
knocking someone upside the head when least expected.

Pick-up Man
someone with optional metrosexual characteristics such as shaved chest
and gelled hair who has studied in the arts of the seduction community
and can employ such subtle psychological strategies as backhanded
compliments and pre-scripted conversations. Works best in the company
of the Wing Man.

Pole Bending
the Cirque du Soleil of the Kama Sutra. Also known as penile puppetry
and genital origami. Can be practiced solo or with a partner.

Poly
multilayered like a wedding cake, born with an extra digit, constructed
from one or more variable and constant, synthetic as neoprene, having
as many corners as sides, the Renaissance ideal, proof that lying causes
side-effects, flared as bell-bottoms, prismatic and multilingual, a blinded
Cyclops, hinged in sections, way too much love for just one person.

Quarter Horse
one half a centaur.

Quit the Cow
marital abandonment.

Rake
　　　　(disambiguation) a lascivious aristocrat during the English
　　　　Restoration (1660-1688) as in Aphra Behn's *The Rover*
　　　　(disambiguation) from orgy to Bedlam in under ten seconds
　　　　(disambiguation) no flop, no drop, otherwise a percentage for
　　　　compensation
to run one's fingers over a patch of skin where once there was hair.

Reata
to have a second Italian meal at the same sitting.

Re-ride
play again for two extra credits.

Rough Stock
bouillon that has sat in the cupboard so long it has fuzzed mold.

Rowel
rut-ro Raggy rand me a rowel! Rats roovy.

Scooter
term of ridicule related to youth or inexperience. As in 'hey scooter, can't keep up with the motorbikes, huh?'

Spur
representing the ACC, it's the Big Fundamental.

Spurring Lick
a salt deposit that contains salmonella.

Star Gazer
aficionado of fuzzbox and 'wall of sound' guitars overdubbed with downtempo sensations of gliding and hovering.

Steer Decorating
recommend upholstery and mildew-resistant slipcovers to brighten a sunroom.

Steer Riding
an oxymoron like a Cherokee Pioneer or freezer burn. See also: ride steering and flag racing.

Stirrups
Gary Glitter, 'The Famous Instigator'.

String
infinitely thin oscillating filaments that reconcile gravitational forces with quantum mechanics.

Suicide Wrap
low density polyethylene film (or a similar material) of not less than 150 micrometers in thickness

Suitcase Handle
back hair aided by chemical stimulants to grow to graspable extremities
Sun Fisher
even on a chariot drawn by seven mares, Suriya was blinded by Sanjna.

Team Roping
tricking the boss into taking the staff out to lunch to discuss new initiatives.

Tie-down Roping
use of straps, harnesses, hogties and padlocks in edge-play; governed by mutually consensual safe-words.

Whipped Down
sleeping in a bed of mashed potatoes.

Wild Drag Race
1. Teri Yaki and her lip-syncing queens use dildos as batons.
2. the xenophobia that lurks at the center of certain reading practices.
3. laying mad rubber down before the Christmas Tree flashes.

Working Cow Horse
milking those udders until you don't hear a drop of moo.

The Presbytery Has Lost None of Its Charm

translation of Jacques Bens with Laurence Petit

The presbytery has lost none of its charm
Nor how a garden's radiance can disarm,
Restoring hand to dog, and bridle to stallion:

But this explanation fails this mystery.

A plague on insight that cracks your talons,
The analysis that dispels your sense of alarm,
Wearing a preposterous cop's cap for a perm,
Pointing out here the just and there the felon.

No explanation can redeem a mystery

I prefer the faded charms of the presbytery
And the sham radiance of a famous garden;
I prefer (it's in my nature) the shuddery
Of fear obliterated by this tiny thief's particularity
To blatancy and fame, like some lamp of Aladdin.

Heirlooms

with Terri Witek

Castle looms blue on the porcelain plate.
Its groves have vanished, along with one crinkly river,

and since the scene no longer requires a knife
this has dropped nearby like a drawbridge.

The window next to a window we know
must be the princess'. Or so we infer

from the blue curtain and a songbird
who seems to expect a palmful of crumbs.

And that something's amiss—
which is to say, in her story,

it rubs between her shoulder blades
or under one ear as she drifts on

her blue bed. Perhaps it's the insignia
under the plate, 'John Cheswick and Sons,

LTD   England///Manhattan',
that so dismays her. But even

to think this makes the blue castle
shake like a trellis as another pattern

(still blue, now above us)
fills with the grit of unseen stars

ubiquitous, unnumbered, so unlike this plate
hoarding dust and dark in a credenza drawer,

along with an alabastrite bust of a Native
American horseman frozen in full gallop,

and cutlery got at an estate sale in Pontefract.
Where there Cheswicks there or their kin?

Jowly boys with gangly limbs, pale girls
who owned closets full of rococo gowns,

her age but happier in that they are imagined?
Blue castles are surrounded by dry moats

in her story, have no recorded history
save the song she hums in rote distraction—

Par dessus nos vertes collines, les montagnes
Au front d'azur, les chaps rayes et les ravines

J'irais d'un vol rapide et sur...
Poulenc's ribald relic passed on

A blue song, scribbled each dusk
into trees that have already gathered

into their own sly clatter two racoons
who aren't afraid of local, dream-laden children

and a platoon of titmice harrowing an owl
who glides down with one seven-tongued sound.

Maybe he's the hero, not some bungling prowler.
The sea's so dark now it's only a murmur

in elsewhere's throat—or so it seems here,
where empty moats thicken into a pattern of brambles

rounding the edge of the world.
But nothing is safe—not the drawer's teardrop handle,

not the hour, not the drift of song lifting
suddenly, like a blue skirt.

Something more lilting than a boned bodice
lined in jacquards, trimmed by crepe de chine,

Yet less mephetic than chrysanthemums
drooping in cut glass until they shrivel

surely as the suggestion of quirky impropriety
secreted away in the minds of old ladies

who swore never to let such insinuation
besmirch their family name, left delicate plates

instead, blue inked, blue-veined, not meant
for canned carrots, better kept wrapped

in terrycloth, never to expose its verso to the stars.
Only along her long limbs, like the scent of sand

after a hard downpour, had the princess
carried off what the ladies could not speak,

a snippet of song broken off, the dim memory
of a castle, the squared jaw of prototypic

handsomeness animated under her fingertips,
a man who broke horses, mounted carriage-wheels,

made his opinions known to the Templar Knights,
spoke softly to dogs when he thought no one saw.

And so what they had been in their world
enters ours, broken by touch,

calling back from leaves curled like fingers
an old sniffer-outer who will drop fragrantly

outside the first junk-shop door.
Plato, hound of the real.

If they're hungry, biscuits and gravy
from white plates in Hunter's Kitchen Cafe

and other doors chiming, loose on their hinges,
even the going-out-of-here-soon's store's,

whose signature goods are already down
to display cases: one waist-high, lit shelf

by shelf, and a taller, revolving one:
$75.00, better money for both.

Here even blue feathers on a stick
(the Candy Castle's owner is dusting

trays in his window) slightly bemuses,
as if summoned from air for a different use,

some other planet's version of reliquary,
a dimension where, were it to exist among

the thumbprints of deep space, they are synchronous
with us, princess and hero, biscuit and gravy,

plate and inscription, two sides of a coin,
the imagined and the real contiguous

and on consignment, smelling of shawl wool and used
appliance. What particles cling to plastic?

What fragments cohere between the blue lines
that turn turret? If the shape of loss

has no shape because it is ongoing, how describe
the way he unfastened her hair from her nape

when both their names, once considered capital,
have washed away, down a crinkly river, vanished?

A whisper is a tendril, is the part of her story
she was never told, though she cannot sleep

when black night turns blue with gathering storm—
soon as it bursts, she's out.

The Falcon

translation of Sebastiano Satta's 'Il Falco' by James Scudamore and Ravi Shankar

High up in the fresh dawn
The golden-eyed falcon
Wheels to and fro on the wind

I worship only one
While you worship a hundred
For you any face will do

The Castle Looms Blue

with Joseph Stanton

1.

The castle looms blue upon the porcelain plate.
A boat—blue, too—sails off-shore,
sinister in its whisper of winds,
while the beautiful daughter and her furtive lover
cross the blue bridge in the porcelain rain
and embrace under the blue willow.

When they look up from their passion
two gigantic birds,
ridiculous in their unlikely warp of wing,
have filled most of the glazed white of the sky
with a verve décoratif.

By the time you have finished
eating the last of the crumbs off the plate
the lovers have achieved their blue consummation,
devoutly, behind the porcelain temple
and sailed off in the blue boat,

while two men—
a wealthy suitor and the girl's father—
watch in azure silence on the pale bridge
as ceramic willow leaves
fall and fall.

2.

Not unlike the snowflakes that settle in drifts,
plowed and salted brown, in Detroit
which has just gone bankrupt, where a couple,
newly married, unpack their belongings
from crates that once held Guatemalan oranges.

Under a framed playbill, a crumpled cat mask,
plaid scarfs and a stack of 45s—Rare Earth,
The Marvelettes, The Contours—the daughter
now turned wife drew from tissue
the very plate that embraced edges of so many knives,

a twisting genetic line of your forbearers,
men with moustaches or stern women in high
collars, whose sketchy sepia toned photos
you may or may not once have seen.
Here she is, fingering the scalloped edge,

with a lacquered thumb tracing the orifice
like inside a shell found at a beach where boats
dot the horizon and enormous seagulls
dive for bluish bits of trash.
By the time you ever crumble a croissant
on the plate, she too will have disappeared.

3.

Because it is Friday night she has placed
their two best plates—
hers with its delicate decoration in blue,
his with its precise red-brown trim—
on the counter of their tiny kitchenette
ready to receive the meal she has prepared,
but her husband, just home from work,
remains oblivious to her pleas
and sits, still in his work attire—
white shirt, black vest, and blue tie.

He is hunched over his newspaper
as if the scores inked on the page
were the reason for his life
within this tight parenthesis
of yellow walls,

where his wife now sits, too,
luminous in her red dress.
She has stopped insisting
and sits by the piano,
plunking the same key
over and over again, a D-sharp

that Edward Hopper can't hear,
staring at the couple from his seat
on the elevated train
sketching them quickly
for a painting he might want to do,

and the wife,
distracted by the rumblings of the train,
begins to pick out the melody of 'Ain't We Got Fun'
and thinks about her blue plate
and how she would like to cruise
away anywhere under its fragile sails.

4.

Not a tableau of a happy chappy
with a hippy whooty, as the dropouts
on the corner contend, snapping
their fingers and beat-boxing freestyle
riffs that contrast with their riches,

or lack thereof, only one of them
ever even having eaten off a real plate.
They band together to shoot dice,
play stoop ball and skully with bottle

caps, anything to waste the hour
before they know they must return
to their women or to a whirlpool
of viscerally swirling downwards
addiction to the bottle or syringe.

The most exact possible transcription
of intimate natural impression,
what Hopper was after in painting
those solitary figures in shadow,
might better need cornet and drums,

music instead of paint to capture
the sheer desperate, frenetic, bluesy
hustle of life in the projects, where a boat
is but a shape on the screen, a piano
only something to hear struck in a pew.

5.

Sometimes I was along for the ride
as he ran his Debit.
Later we would veer over to Forest Park
to fish tight-line off the side of a blue boat.

A castle abandoned after a World's Fair
loomed blue on the horizon,
its ramparts catching
late afternoon light.

Our lines would sing
every little melody of current,
refrain of rock, delicate trill of fish nibble.
It was a tune the string made
against the unmoving finger;
the instrument playing its soloist.

With finger on string we could feel
to the depths of watery places.
We could sit for hours,
catching little
beyond glimpsed landscapes.
Sometimes he only watched the line,

but I liked to rest my finger on the string
so I could gaze at the other boats
or the deft red-winged blackbirds
and their awkward young
zig-zigging tight lines
from ground to sky to tree.

We spoke no more
than did the water or the clouds
drifting in the breeze.

6.

Glimpsed in flashes off the highway, a medieval jawbone
sketch of crags against the skyline, then river between trees

and car, car, car as usual. Early mornings, alone with radio,
you drive this stretch, and on some days startle at the sudden

vista of another century, the conjuration of arrow loops,
crenellations, machicolations and murder holes, a barbarism

that on closer inspection reveals itself to be a simulation
of the medieval, the quirky former residence of the stage actor

who brought the deerstalker cap, tweed Inverness cape
and Calabash pipe to Sherlock Holmes. Sir William Gillette

who designed a fieldstone home in the German Rhineland-
style, a gnarled knuckle of a mansion that allowed him to spy

on his guests with elaborate mirrors, escape through trick
doors, and ride a train with guests like Charlie Chaplin around

his estate. The Nutmeg State is full of estates thinking nautical
thoughts of birds and yachts upon the Sound, but the inner

cities of Hartford, Bridgeport and New Haven stay parched
places, bereft of porcelain plates and bobbing blue boats.

When Gillette died, without an heir, he precluded possession
of his land by any 'blithering sap-head who has no conception

of where he is or with what surrounded.' You must confess
then to having no clue about what special form of depthlessness

and difference this drive each morning passes you through,
where you can see castles and panhandlers mere minutes apart,

where the Connecticut River swells from Quebec to Long Island,
and where at the end of the day, you will start it all over again.

7.

At night it seemed a house in dark, fairytale woods
so high were the maples and oaks in every yard.

By day it was just another suburb
wedged between railroad tracks and expressways,
paths of desperate transit to the desperate city,
desperately needed because Long Island is so long.

But most nights blue napkins rested on a rosewood table,
and we ate off the good china with your ancient, Irish mother
who loved the colour blue so much that you made sure
the walls of her room and all its furnishings remained
in that rarest of colors even decades after her passing.

So hard now to remember you
and your red hair,
and those ornate plates, so long gone, too.

8.

Wisps spilling from a passel,
floating spirits in the form of flickering lights
in the evening sky just barely visible
beyond the curtain's lace edge
stained a faint lentil bean colour.

The alcazar of the stars serrates depth
with waves particulate as sand-grains
if impossible to hold in the hand.
Sounds an open palm might make
passing through the twilight air.

However we happened here, forged
from reptile, neuron and pure want,
vaster realms populate space beyond us,
the castle a plate to eat forms from,
full of conjecture plum-ripened in the sun.

The Theory of Radioactivity

with Brian Turner

Burnt-out taxis rest like lozenges on a tongue of rain
in Phnom Penh, where the suctioned geckos stare for hours
at the zigzag tiles of the *Commissariat's* roof, double zeros
doubled back in pools spooled around sandstone fingers
pointed at the pastlife of stars, the ornately carved *prangs*
of Angkorian temples clenching open a cool space to pray
under distant frigatebirds that ride among streets of clouds,
their wings in a tropospheric heat as Bikini Atoll
lifts the year 1952 in a column of ash, snow
of calcite and coral to follow, the drift and falling
chunks of archipelago vaporising into thin air
on eternal patrol with vague whispery outlines of hands
that anchored an array of destroyers, a show of strength.
Now the coconuts on palms still suffused with cesium
glow faintly at night like phosphorescent bowling balls
or the eyes of sailfish and skipjacks once hooked
and pulled hard through the blue current of eternity,
as we all are and will be, our ears filling with white
noise like a purely theoretical construction, a solar flare
that ejects through space ions of unknowable unknowing.

Tempo Rubato Luminoso Con Moto
or: Notes from The Field Guide of Post-Lapsarian Instruction

with Lisa Russ Spaar

The woodpecker's catechism, doctrinal, drilling the house,
is the discordance between thinking and thought,
is the candelabra of your hand, there, effacing thought,
is the clock's cluck-clucking: *What is the chief end of man?*
Like egg whites into batter, each mammal brain furrowing
folds in layers better to fit the fetal growth—rapid, bastular—
leaving petroglyphs of spidery, chromosomal pictograms
abraded deep into grooved walls for your someday
senescent mind to decipher. Please, your hand again.
There. There, there. Another furrow of knowing.
What rule hath God given to direct us? Inklings, and so forth.

O, pileated hammerer of post, oak, rood,
making feast of this attic dormer, *what reason have you
for saying so?* Seconds eat seconds from your palm,
another grain in the sand mandala the wind whisks,
itself whittled raw by such unseen imminance
that each shape pours from a glass to be absorbed.
A: *You shall have no other gods.* Q: *What does this mean?*
I have seen your body pendant with eon.
The desire-devoured story; the roof given wings.
There. Not there. Like silt and ash from consideration
of fire, on fingertips the catechesis of the fossil bed.

Two Water Towers Red (2008)

...a sliver of light hitting the street at an angle...
—*Sonya Sklaroff*

as	in
what	dusk
passes	through

how the weight of the not-yet-night-sky upon the rooftops
pushes down upon the thrust of cornice and spire, the light
interpenetrates   ochers like red clay   dug out from
loam with hand   axe or mattock yet   is the reverse
of earth being firmament, not firm but atmospheric, some-
how invisible from the sidewalks most of the time walkers
walk by with their dogs on a leash or their ears plugged up
with music then   suddenly, up ahead   everything lit
up with bonfire   you can never think   how you did
not notice before. Think Toni Morrison in *Jazz* describing
the citysky emptying itself of surface, 'more like the ocean
than the ocean itself', so close you could pluck it, a peach
made of scattered light, fine particles born from interstellar
collisions, while   the deepening glow   grows redder
in dream-space   exhuming a buried   rhythm   beat
from footfall, taxis, curling stream, pigeons, the shuttered
windows flickering with television, fluctuating in shadow
as bodies pass by, all of it rising up and up to meet what's
falling, pulled earthwards by gravity until an equilibrium
so ephemeral it cannot last longer than minutes arrives to
stretch boundless light: the whole city as living organism

The Perils of Homecoming

with Priya Sarukkai Chabria

The castle looms blue upon the porcelain plate,
the shepherdess rests within the coffee cup's gilt,
palm-sized Pierrot sits Pierrette on his knee for a kiss
her ceramic tutu ruffled by his haste while inches
away The Pied Piper leads his rats of silvery clay:
this menagerie once within memory's chamfered glass
bolts, for pain's insoluble grains gargle up the throat
in an inverse pantomime of tongue and tract. Such flow
of grief cannot be digested or broken down by bile
but persists moment after lifetime after era,
an inheritance of malady the mask of which a pale
face wears as persuasively as the ochre, the dead
as inexorably as the unborn alas! The Cumaean sibyl
peers (more granules than limbs) from her bell
jar on the shelf and whispers I want to die!
Weighted by knowledge's intractable metamorphoses
into light as the body shrinks. Around
her ampulla glitter shards of promises, illusions
lost, broken rings of love, the salver of desire
beyond salvaged. Yet all's not lost, perhaps. Aren't
all dichotomies birthed from a whole? Squint.
Unpeel eyes. Flurry the dust. What's
that burning, burning, burning, burning sensation
like the smashed up bits of asteroids and comets
orbiting a planet to retrace a path hewn from prophecy
in a self-reflexive knot or biofeedback loop. Circulatory
ouroboros of eternal return where a serpent eats its own
tail. Just so, each of us a gravitational body around
which our past rotates—faces of lovers, shards of toys
we once imagined alive, the cave of a hundred

openings where songs take the shape of oak leaves,
where we may have played in this or that lifetime,
and where we may yet play again.
Yet the cool smoothness of porcelain,
the grains of gold gilt beneath blind finger tips, the dust
on Pierrette's net tutu of glass that shadows touch—what's
this lust that burns into bones, what's this we cannot
turn back on, tail in our mouths, we who are toys
of eternal return? What's this grief, this wonder, this
mesh of clay, colour, fire that constructs our glass, this
brokenness that bleeds prayer?

Ephemerality = Permanence

with Lena Kallergi

Each reading of your palm a different road
verging from soil and forking into possibilities
in a wild and foreign ocean
no vaster than the line it makes with the sky
changing with touch
to resemble a soap bubble's rim—
how it trails, surfaces illusion,
peppers translucence with lids
of water underneath the skin
layered with centuries of silt and smelt—
sea of the past, rivers of tomorrow
branch backwards in tributaries that
cannot be named and will not stay.
I know no secret that won't sail away
so come with me, where
no knot not nautical in nature
binds us like twisting sheets to a cleat.

Last Turn on the Left

with Clare Rossini

Yes, Lycra can improve your performance
but that little red sports car, only its music could tell you where it's off to,
a vineyard in the foothills, a Rosh Hashanah Seder, or a cliff's edge,
its mids and woofers growling with guitar or languid with opera.
And when you get to where you thought your thought was leading you,
that note-smeared testament nobody can pin to a latitude
you'll find the excrement of grief, its uncontrolled movement
of leave-taking, every arrival latent with its own departure,
like the Buddhist sutra on the mindfulness of the body in decay
sung by ancient Indian pilgrims in the charnel grounds
where a corpse still green, still held together by sinew,
becomes the bespattered subject of contemplation
Where does an hour go? Same place as a life.
I thought I was following this wending road toward the sea's
terminal blues, thought the heart was taking me there
by its weight and chill. I thought I was being led.

Thiruppavai: The Path to Krishna

translation of Andal

It's the eighth month of the new year, *Marghazi*,
and the moon is full, *mun-pani*, early dew, beading
on the grass, offering moisture to the air, a sign
of all good things to come.

Let's bathe dear *gopis*, sing hymns to *Ayarpati*,
relish this rich land with our loosened limbs,
embody the bliss of simply being together
with the son of *Nandagopa*.

Around his face, the cosmos revolves, glinting
starlight from his spear, the lion-cub of Yasoda
fierce yet lotus-eyed, dark-hued yet resplendent
with the joy of all creation.

Let the world consider the rituals of our vows,
sing the songs we sing, smell the jasmine strung
into a garland to praise the one who steals *ghee*
from my mouth as blessing.

Rub the kohl from my eyes, scour the flower-scent
from my body, show me as I am to him, an elemental
offering not good, not bad, but simply present.
Show him as he is to me.

In flooded fields of red paddy, carp leap into flight
that doesn't last, yet won't subside, and spotted
beetles graze our eyelashes as we splash our song
heavenward for liberation.

We sing the many names of the world-encircler,
drawing promises in sand that if we might please
him, the rains will fall, honeybees teem, and udders
will groan to fill our pots.

Let the sky open with water to cleanse us for him,
splintering the fog with lightening, imbuing
the cosmic holy Yamuna with flow and overflow
from the syllables of his name.

King of eternal Mathura of the North, yogis chant
his name after years of penance, but we cow-girls
who churn buttermilk with tamarind hands know
no better than how to rejoice.

May his grace rain like a shower of arrows where
we bathe, awakening the sleeping ones with thunder
and cow-stink, no less pure for being themselves.
We come to him the same way.

He is the peacock of the woods, who brightened
his mother's womb and whose very skin is supple
as a cobra's hood, glistening as if basted in almond
oil and we just can't look away.

May our past crimes burn, let those yet to come
burn and turn to ash, know us only as we are before
you now, cowgirls bathing in what pours from above,
what rises from below to soak us.

Do you not hear dear friends how the birds chirrup,
how resonant the conch sounds from the temple
of Garuda's lord? It pervades the air with his name—
Hari. Hari. Hari. Hurry.

Isn't it so that our stems exist only for a blossom
to open? Don't you hear how his name seems
to cool us when it enters our mind? Beautiful
maidens, open your doors.

So the sky each morning brightens into dawn,
the buffaloes seek their own space to graze,
and we await him Sleeping friend, rouse from
your slumber to sing again.

No matter what gems' luster or frankincense
fragrance lulls you to sleep, no matter how soft
your bed, how sumptuous the trappings of home,
we are here singing his names.

Shuck off the husk of your weariness, step outside
of dream and join us to praise the elusive one,
Madhava, the rapturous lord of Vaikuntha.
Shake off your sleep to live!

The udders of the buffaloes are bursting with milk,
just thinking of their calves, they wet the floors
with hopefulness, the same fervor that grips us
as we knock on your door.

Even Venus has arisen from Jupiter and we wash
ourselves while you still sleep, your lidded eyes
dark as a bee burrowed into a sticky hidden bud.
The lucky day begs you wake.

In the pond, the lotus blooms and other blossoms
purpled delicate lips open. *Saddhus* in ochre robes
and bone-white teeth blow the conch to signal
our bridegroom has arrived!

We are all gathered here together in throaty song,
praising the mighty one who killed the demon
elephant, the limitless one who spans the worlds,
lit from within like sapphire.

The lamps blaze while you still laze in bed, still
dreaming even when roosters crow their crooked tune,
even while we finger the *table*, pounding forth time—
strip off fatigue, come with us!

Squint your half-open lotus eyes into the elliptical
mouths of *kinkini* bells. His gaze goes everywhere
but when it falls on us, all of our worry disappears.
Can you hear how he nears?

Like a lion flinging his mane rashly in a mountain
cave, stretching his muscular length into full roar,
he too has awakened to the glory of all creation
in another monsoon season.

We praise his feet that measured worlds, his hands
that hoisted a mountain range as an umbrella.
We praise his spear, his leather-skin *parai*-drum,
His strength and his music.

Come forth from seclusion, we call to him, out
into the light where we play, float by on a banyan
leaf to scatter shower petals on us poor girls
who long for his blessings.

O splendid Govinda, for him we drape ourselves
in silk, pin our hair, put on earrings and anklets,
steep rice in so much *ghee* it drips down elbows:
so much sweetness, this life.

We know that we are artless innocents, simple
village cowgirls, nothing more or less, yet the bond
between us and the faultless one is unbreakable,
forged from endlessness itself.

Though unthinkable, he too was born just like us
and to him we say, we are yours and yours alone,
made to serve you and to worship at your feet.
This is the prayer we cast into air.

So Kotai threaded this garland of thirty stanzas
about the moon-bright *gopis* who loved Madhava
and anyone who recites these verses even today
will incarnate joyfulness forever.

Afterword

It's rare to glean a chance to remix one's oeuvre, but that's exactly the chance I have been given by Recent Work Press. It is, therefore, a profound joy to present you with my new and selected poems taken from my published books in North America and India, beginning with *Instrumentality* (Cherry Grove, 2004); *Wanton Textiles* (No Tell Motel, 2006); *Language for a New Century* (W.W. Norton & Co., Inc, 2008); *Seamless Matter* (Rain Taxi/Ohm Editions, 2010); *Voluputuous Bristle* (Finishing Line Press, 2010); *Deepening Groove* (National Poetry Review, 2011); *What Else Could it Be* (Carolina Wren, 2015); *The Autobiography of a Goddess* (Zubaan Books/University of Chicago Press, 2017); and *Durable Transit* (Poetrywala, 2018). However, instead of being listed in chronological or alphabetical order, these poems from the last twenty years are constellated together, in retrospect and with consideration, around seven primary themes: *Homage*, or that long-standing post-Virgillian tradition of celebrating those works and creators, from John Cage and Prince, to Ovid and Frida Kahlo, who have provided my own life aesthetic pleasure (and measure); *Pataphysics*, that (very French) tendril of philosophy that deals with an imaginary realm beyond metaphysics and provides a space where, as Alan Watts puts it, we become an aperture through which the universe looks at and explores itself; *Singularities*, or the recasting of identity politics as something much more potential and expansive, like the curvature of space-time into that one-dimensional point where density and gravity become infinite, and where the laws of physics and rhetoric begin equally to break down; *Voyages*, those trips to cities and towns around the world that have shifted something inside me enough to spur their varied memorialisation in language; *Post-pastorals* which refer back to the pastoral tradition but reach through into a conceptual ecology that makes each observer complicit in what is observed; *Carnal Nature*, our heaving, sensual breath of lyric body made manifest in shapely lines to intone until we can groan in mutual bloom; and *Phrase and Contour*, which is as close to being an improvisational musician as I will ever come, jamming with writers as varied as Eileen Myles, Jim Daniels, Alvin Pang, Rodger Kamentz, and Google, and translating Sardinian poet Sebastiano

Satta with James Scudamore and ancient Tamil goddess Andal with Priya Sarukkai Chabria. I end on this note of exultation, exiting with a multi-vocal patchwork rock opera verbal tableau meant to hum in your ears when you put down this book.

—Ravi Shankar / Mumbai, India (February 2018)

Notes

p.37, Title is taken from a phrase in O'Henry's 'The Skylight Room', (Henry, O. *Tales of O. Henry.* New York: Doubleday & Co., 1969.) that describes the aforementioned room: 'In it was an iron cot, a washstand and a chair. A shelf was the dresser. Its four bare walls seemed to close in upon you like the sides of a coffin. Your hand crept to your throat, you gasped, you looked up as from a well-- and breathed once more. Through the glass of the little skylight you saw a square of blue infinity.'

p.39, From 'The Furnished Room'. Henry, O. The Complete Works of O. Henry. New York: Doubleday & Co., 1936.

About the cover

'Shadow of Darshan IV' by GR Iranna, © 2012.

GR Iranna was born in 1970, Sindgi, Bijapur, Karnataka, India. During his youth, Iranna studied in a Gurukul (a system of education where the student resides with the teacher) and lived in an ashram for almost seven years. This helped to form a strong connection to his cultural roots, which enters his work alongside his exploration of the antitheses of inherent dualities of the world. Iranna endeavors to translate an internal landscape onto tactile surfaces and aspects of Buddhist art influences are evident. Although he began painting oil on canvases, Iranna later developed his range of medium, embarking on his now primary use of tarpaulin. The artist lives and works in New Delhi, India.

https://irannagr.com/

Ravi Shankar is author/editor of a dozen books, including most recently *Durable Transit: New and Selected Poems, The Golden Shovel: New Poems Honoring Gwendolyn Brooks* and *Autobiography of a Goddess,* translations of the 9th century Tamil poet/saint, Andal and winner of the 2016/2017 Muse India Translation Prize. He co-edited W.W. Norton's *Language for a New Century,* called 'a beautiful achievement for world literature' by Nobel laureate Nadine Gordimer and founded one of the world's oldest online journals of arts, *Drunken Boat.* He has won a Pushcart Prize and held fellowships from the MacDowell Colony, the Corporation of Yaddo, and the Rhode Island Commission on the Arts. His work has appeared in *The New York Times, The Paris Review, The Financial Times,* and on National Public Radio, the BBC and on PBS. He has been interviewed and translated into over 10 languages, and he currently holds a research fellowship from the University of Sydney.

Praise for Ravi Shankar

To read Ravi Shankar is to be steeped deeper in the dangerous and delightful, ruthless and sacred nature of things. These poems, new and old, find idioms, forms and rhythms that order, a while, the chaos that stalks and calls us all. Here, is the frantic, shapely world of thought and thing and almost fathomless feeling. Like Wallace Stevens, Shankar manages both to mean and unsettle meaning in every other line.
—Mark Tredinnick, author of *Fire Diary* and winner of the Montreal International Poetry Prize

The role of clocks, the magic of Prince, the art of Chagall, sex, science, the language of nature and the nature of language, India, America, politics, and love—there seemingly is nothing beyond the ken or pen of this polymath poet. Ravi Shankar's poetry is thoughtful and quotable, dense with allusion and metaphor and yet airy and light of foot. It's a rare combination of the erudite and the approachable. Playful, erotic, witty and wise.
—Linda Jaivin, author of *The Empress Lover*

Ravi Shankar's poetry starts with the Rig Veda, and moves away from Sanscrit to the most modern voices: from English to French to American. Ravi Shankar knows how to play his chosen instrument, poetry, better than anyone, and he allows the instrument to play its soloist too.
— John Tranter. author of *Urban Myths*, *Starlight*, and *Heart Starter.*

Ravi Shankar is now, truly, one of America's finest younger poets.
—Dick Allen, Connecticut poet laureate

Ravi Shankar's *Seamless Matter*, when read as a whole, becomes nothing less than a praise song of our shared physicality, and of existence known, as it must be, under the scepter of time.
—Jane Hirshfield, Chancellor of the Academy of American Poets

Ravi Shankar's poems are the verbal artifacts of a singular, many-sided and distinguished consciousness.
—Vijay Seshadri, Pulitzer Prize winner

Quirky, quizzical, inquisitive, by turns lyrical and meditative, Ravi Shankar's poems are guided by a strong intelligence toward resolutions that are both surprising and apt.
—Gregory Orr, Rockefeller Fellow

Those to whom poetry is essential as the supreme use of language will ... have the opportunity to discover how the poet outreaches everything prose can illuminate in who and what we are, no matter where, on the map. Tina Chang, Nathalie Handal and Ravi Shankar have boldly envisaged and compiled a beautiful achievement for world literature.
–Nadine Gordimer, Nobel Prize winner

Shankar collaborates with both painters and with other contemporary poets by finding the zone and bringing 'new forms of elasticity into being.'
—Rae Armantrout, Pulitzer Prize winner

Ravi Shankar's poems are filled with the pleasure of subjects dissolving into ideas, ideas folding into sounds, and sounds echoing familiar but elusive translocations.
—Charles Bernstein, Fellow of the American Academy of Arts & Sciences

Ravi Shankar is a postmodern flâneur. He wanders the world's real and fictional gridded cities (or perhaps his astral body swoops high above them) and reports back.
—Amy Gerstler, National Book Critics Circle Award winner

It's the language itself that does the trick—Shankar has a marvelous way of getting sound and phrasing to say both something and themselves.
    —Cole Swensen, Guggenheim Fellow

2018 Editions
The Uncommon Feast **Eileen Chong**
Inlandia **KA Nelson**
Peripheral Vision **Martin Dolan**
Ley Lines and the Rustling of Cedar **Niloofar Fanaiyan**
The Love of the Sun **Matt Hetherington**
Moving Targets **Jen Webb**
Things I Have Thought to Tell You Since I Saw You Last **Penelope Layland**
The Many Uses of Mint **Ravi Shankar**
Abstractions **Various**

2017 Editions
A Song, the World to Come **Miranda Lello**
Cities: Ten Poets, Ten Cities **Various**
The Bulmer Murder **Paul Munden**
Dew and Broken Glass **Penny Drysdale**
Members Only **Melinda Smith** and **Caren Florance**
the future, un-imagine **Angela Gardner** and **Caren Florance**
Proof **Maggie Shapley**
Black Tulips **Moya Pacey**
Soap **Charlotte Guest**
Isolator **Monica Carroll**
Ikaros **Paul Hetherington**
Work & Play **Owen Bullock**

all titles available from
www.recentworkpress.com

RECENT
WORK
PRESS

CPSIA information can be obtained
at www.ICGtesting.com
Printed in the USA
FSHW011153040221
78215FS